GREAT
BUILDING SUCCESS
IDEAS

Dr Peter Shaw

D1366662

mc **Marshall Cavendish**
Business

1 New Industrial Road, Singapore 536196
genrefsales@sg.marshallcavendish.com
www.marshallcavendish.com/genref

Other Marshall Cavendish Offices:
Marshall Cavendish Corporation. 99 White Plains Road, Tarrytown NY 10591-9001, USA • Marshall Cavendish International (Thailand) Co Ltd. 253 Asoke, 12th Flr, Sukhumvit 21 Road, Klongtoey Nua, Wattana, Bangkok 10110, Thailand • Marshall Cavendish (Malaysia) Sdn Bhd, Times Subang, Lot 46, Subang Hi-Tech Industrial Park, Batu Tiga, 40000 Shah Alam, Selangor Darul Ehsan, Malaysia.

Marshall Cavendish is a trademark of Times Publishing Limited

National Library Board, Singapore Cataloguing-in-Publication Data
Names: Shaw, Peter, author.
Title: 100 Great Building Success Ideas / Dr Peter Shaw.
Description: Singapore : Marshall Cavendish Business, 2016.
Identifiers: OCN 932261775 | ISBN 978-981-46-7782-0 (paperback)
Subjects: LCSH: Success--Psychological aspects. | Success in business. | Career development. | Self-management (Psychology)
Classification: LCC HF5386 | DDC 650.1--dc23

Printed in Singapore by Markono Print Media Pte Ltd

This book is dedicated to Professor Gerald Blake,
an outstanding geographer who taught at Durham University.
He has been a key influence on me at moments of decision,
always combining clarity of thinking and
calmness of approach.

CONTENTS

Section C: Address what might hold you back

Section D: Generate forward momentum

Section E: Handle setbacks with care

Section F: Build your reputation

Section G: Balance the short term and the long term

Section H: Sustain the success

Section I: Grow team success

Section J: Engage with the future

ACKNOWLEDGEMENTS

As I LOOK BACK OVER 67 years of life I am indebted to many different people who have helped shape my thinking about what success means. At secondary school David Rhodes inspired me as a geographer. John Lepper enabled me to think through the balance between academic study, faith issues and community responsibility.

At Durham University Gerald BIake and George Smith enabled me to reflect on opportunities beyond university. Gerald Blake, a Geography Professor, set me off in the direction of Regent College, Vancouver. George Smith, my College Vice-Principal, encouraged me to enter Government service. At Regent College, where I did a master's degree in Christian Studies, Jim Houston and Ward Gasque inspired me to bring together aspirations about work, community and faith.

At the start of my 32 years working within the UK Government Hugh Jenkins, Sheila Browne and Jim Hamilton helped shape my thinking about the contribution I could make as a public servant. Working closely with politicians I respected, such as Mark Carlisle, Keith Joseph, Kenneth Baker, David Blunkett and David Miliband, helped reinforce the importance of keeping in reasonable balance seeking success and nourishing a hinterland that kept me sane in the most demanding times.

Robin Linnecar and Bob Goodall helped to shape my entry into executive coaching in 2003, shifting my mind-set to see success as all about other people's success. Those who supported my writing have played an important part on my journey. Rob Innes encouraged me to write my first booklet in 2004. Caroline Armitage commissioned me to write my first book, *Conversation Matters*. John Pritchard has always been a great source of encouragement. Christine Smith and

Melvin Neo have been encouraging in prompting me to develop new ideas for books.

I am grateful to my colleagues at Praesta Partners, who always provide constructive ideas about how best to enable individuals to build success and overcome setbacks. Jackie Tookey typed the manuscript with great efficiency. Sonia John-Lewis has managed my diary and time effectively in order to enable me to write. Melvin Neo has been a thoughtful editor of this series. Justin Lau has been an admirable editor of this book. Zoe Stear gave me valuable suggestions as I shaped the topics to be covered in the book.

I am grateful to Matthew Coats, who has written the foreword to this book. Matthew has brought a determined and pragmatic approach in a sequence of leadership roles. We have often reflected on what success does or does not mean. I am grateful to Matthew for sharing his thoughts in the foreword on what building success means to him.

In writing this book I have drawn from my first career working in the public sector for 32 years and then a second career working in the private sector for 13 years, alongside a variety of roles within the voluntary sector. It has been a privilege to draw from the experience of working with leaders across six continents in a wide range of settings. I am indebted to a range of people for sharing ideas about what success has meant or not meant for them.

Most of the manuscript was written in a wooden hut at the end of our garden in Godalming, away from the distractions of the computer and the telephone. Some chapters were written in Bowness, overlooking Lake Windermere, and in Ayrshire, looking towards the hills of Arran.

Frances, my wife, has been hugely supportive. I am indebted to her and our three children and their spouses, who regularly tease me and bring me firmly back to earth. I am indebted to my mother, who was widowed when I was seven. She taught me that success is always about enabling others to overcome their own inner obstacles and living contentedly and calmly with whatever happens to you.

I am grateful to you, the reader, for the time you are committing to dip into the ideas in the book. I hope they give you some useful pointers about what success might mean or not mean for you going forward.

FOREWORD

BUILDING SUCCESS, like building anything else, takes time, energy, patience and commitment. It is a team activity too, and I have always liked collaborations that aim for mutual success. This book is full of fantastic examples of how to build success. I thought I would open it with some reflections on the essential ingredients for success and how we can put values into effect.

I am delighted to see Peter turning his attention to one of the big themes of the moment. He has built success throughout his civil service career, and more recently as a leading coach and thinker he has helped many leaders to do the same.

Over the last 20 years I've learnt a lot about leadership – more often from the things that didn't go so well. I have concluded that in the end it's about creating the right environment for others to give their best. It's about giving broad direction and supporting people to get there, particularly when the going is tough.

I have seen plenty of examples of things that have gone well, and plenty that haven't. There's no magic formula, but the common features of success are threefold.

Firstly, leaders who are authentic do not hide behind job titles, structures or governance. The most successful leaders are the ones who take the time to understand and connect with the people they work with, and who are not afraid to show uncertainty or vulnerability. They adopt a holistic approach, always try to see the whole picture, and are not afraid to ask when they don't know.

Secondly, it is essential to have the right people behaving in the right way involved in a team endeavour. The most successful people will always invest in and nurture their team. Creating real success means allowing others to succeed too. It's really not necessary to try to prove that you are the smartest person in the room. The real skill is to let others shine and achieve their potential.

Thirdly, leaders who manage to sustain success are usually comfortable in their own skin. They know what drives them and what holds them back. Great leaders find ways of building personal and organisational resilience. There is a synergy between their personal and professional values, and a hinterland of wider interests which enables them to keep a balanced perspective. A successful life is about more than just success at work.

One of my personal passions is creating the conditions for success in an organisation. A lot of this centres on developing a culture that is positive and outward-looking, and on making sure that line management is first-rate. I think everyone realises that a line manager can make all the difference in someone's experience of an organisation.

I also want to leave behind the outdated concepts of a fixed workplace and fixed working patterns. In organisations I play a part in, I want flexible working with technology that supports it as a basic part of everyone's job.

Fairness is also of great importance to me. No organisation can hope to succeed if it does not embrace and promote diversity and inclusion. Fairness extends to performance management and demonstrable equal treatment. All of these things play a part in creating successful organisations, but what matters most is trust and common purpose. If you have these then you are well on the way to building success.

Those of you reading this book will be from a wide range of organisations in different countries. There will be lots of differences, but something that unites all organisations is that good leadership builds success. I hope you enjoy the book. Peter has collected some great ideas about building success which I hope will inspire you to come up with, and put into practice, some of your own.

Matthew Coats
Director General
Ministry of Justice
London

INTRODUCTION

WHEN WALKING RECENTLY along the River Ayr Way I was hoping to see an occasional kingfisher. Suddenly I spotted a hint of blue on a rock in the river. I knew for certain that it was a kingfisher when the elegant bird flew down the river with its blue plumage reflecting in the sunlight. Seeing this kingfisher was a delightful surprise. It was an unexpected and welcome moment of success.

A couple of years earlier, when I had been walking along the Ribble Way, I strayed off the route accidentally. I decided to take a shortcut – over some wet ground – to rejoin the route. To my surprise the mud was deep and I sank to hip level. If I did not do something quickly there was a risk of my disappearing into this quicksand. I managed to scoop out the mud around one leg and lift myself flat onto the mud and then crawl to solid ground. Getting stuck in the mud and feeling for a moment that I could sink into oblivion was an unpleasant surprise. Success was crawling out of that situation, reaching safety and being able to complete the walk.

Success might be a delightful, unexpected surprise, or it might be about survival through demanding or difficult times. Success might mean different things at different stages of life. Success in your twenties might be about finding a job or a spouse. In your thirties it might be about progressing in your chosen career. In your forties it might be about living harmoniously with teenagers. In your fifties it might be about balancing a range of different responsibilities. In your sixties it might be about using those golden years to best effect through a range of activities. In your seventies it might be passing on your wisdom to your grandchildren. In your eighties it might be about coping with physical and mental limitations. In your nineties it might be about surviving and trying to keep a smile on your face.

This book is about building success across different areas of your life. I encourage you to lay the foundations for success across the whole of life. The ideas in the book are intended to form a basis for you to be successful in whatever are your chosen activities. For many it will be in paid work, but for others it will be in voluntary activity. Success across the whole of life depends on holding on to a balance about what is important to you, covering your family, community, culture, faith and work.

As you seek to build success I encourage you to:

- Be willing to seek success, and if it comes sit lightly to it

- Be willing to take responsibility and not run away from accountability

- Encourage others to be successful and see your mentoring of them as part of your success

- Accept that success means different things at different times of your life

- Be ready to move on if success does not come or if your success begins to erode

- Accept that despite all your best efforts the success you seek does not always happen

Building success requires commitment, energy and an open mind. It involves listening to others and distilling their perspectives and advice. Building success involves shaping ideas, testing boundaries, building alliances and learning from what works and does not work.

This book provides prompts for thought on balancing priorities well, understanding the drivers of your ambition, addressing what might hold you back, generating forward momentum, handling setbacks with care, building your reputation, balancing the short term and the long term, sustaining the success, growing team success and engaging with the future.

The book is designed so you can dip into the different sections. It is intended to be a practical tool both for individuals and for those mentoring younger people.

My encouragement to you is to spend some time developing clarity in your own mind about what building success means for you. I hope that the ideas in the book will provide prompts for thought as you review what success means to you in different areas and stages of your life.

Professor Peter Shaw, CB, PhD, DCL (Hon)
Godalming, England
peter.shaw@praesta.com

SECTION A
BALANCE PRIORITIES WELL

WHAT MATTERS MOST TO YOU IN LIFE?

YOUR HONEST ANSWER to the question of what matters most to you in life provides an essential framework for decisions on priorities.

The idea

What matters most to us will vary depending on our situation and stage of life. If we are hungry and have nowhere to live our top priorities will be about food and shelter. If we are isolated and alone what matters most might be human contact and intimacy.

We all have physical, emotional, intellectual and spiritual needs. If one of these areas is starved we can become dissatisfied and disorientated. If our basic physical and emotional needs are met the pursuit of intellectual or spiritual ideas becomes much more important.

In the hothouse of a work environment what can matter most is being successful and being seen to be successful at work. When we are immersed in our families the most important consideration is the healthy development of our children. When we are immersed in a sport we can be completely preoccupied with doing the sport to the best of our ability.

A key starting point in thinking about what success means for us is the answer to the question, 'What matters most to me in my life?' What is the desired mix between family, community and work? What is the balance between physical, emotional, intellectual and spiritual wellbeing that is most important to us? Where does career success fit in relation to our community contribution, or our family wellbeing?

Veronique grew up in a family where both her parents were very supportive of her education and were ambitious for her. With a good degree, Veronica entered Government service. She had a strong commitment to public service values and worked effectively on successive projects. Her friends did not see as much of her as they would have liked and thought that Veronique always put her work first. Veronique was reluctant to enter into deep relationships at a personal level because she did not want to be diverted from her career. When she repeatedly got home at 9 p.m. or later, after rewarding but tiring days, she began to wonder whether she had got her priorities quite right.

In practice

- What matters most to you in life at the moment?

- What do you think will be most important to you in five years' time?

- How well are you able to balance your physical, intellectual, emotional and spiritual needs?

WHAT MATTERS MOST TO THOSE WHO ARE CLOSEST TO YOU?

Balancing priorities well includes taking account of what matters most to those who are closest to you, or else they will cease to be so close to you.

The idea

If someone is in awe of you or loves you deeply they may subjugate their needs and preferences to yours. Any successful, sustained relationship will involve putting the needs of another person first, but if it is always one person's needs and preferences which are subjugated, then it is likely to be a challenge to sustain the long-term quality of the relationship.

As you seek to build your success it is important to recognise who is most precious to you and find out what is most important for their equilibrium and wellbeing. If you and a prospective partner are equally ambitious there are major questions to be answered if you are going to maintain a relationship and potentially a family whilst both continue to pursue those ambitions. If what matters most to your children is your presence at key moments in their lives, then practical decisions have to be made and stuck to.

What matters is an openness to the preferences of significant others and a willingness to plan ahead and make sacrifices, alongside a recognition that nobody's preferences are always going to be met. There may be seasons when one person's preferences are met more readily.

What is important is that over a longer period there is an acknowledgement of what matters most to those who are closest to you.

Veronique enjoyed working closely with Ben, a colleague in another part of Government. They met for a drink after work on a couple of occasions and decided to go for a long walk one Saturday. Veronique began to explore with Ben what interests they had in common. Veronique and Ben were at an early stage of finding out what was most important to them. Veronique warmed to Ben but was wary about whether she wanted the time commitment of an intimate relationship.

In practice

- How much do you care about what matters most to members of your family?

- How do you keep up to date in appreciating what matters most to family members and close friends?

- As you build new friendships and relationships, how do you find out discreetly about the needs and preferences of new friends?

WHAT GIVES YOU MOST FULFILMENT?

It is important to be honest with yourself about what gives you most fulfilment and to use that as a touchstone in deciding on priorities.

The idea

The completion of certain activities gives us huge personal satisfaction. This might be cooking a delicious meal, or growing large carrots, or hitting a stunning return of serve in a tennis match. There are moments when we get a sense of achievement from something relatively incidental and transitory. These moments of fulfilment are essential for our day-to-day wellbeing; they can also give us clues about how best we might use our talents and preferences to the benefit of the organisations of which we are a part.

The individual who has a sense of achievement when they have written a work proposal is likely to be fulfilled writing more complicated proposals on more substantive issues. The individual who discovers that they can motivate a team well is in a great position to offer to lead teams with increasingly demanding remits.

After completing different types of activity it can be helpful to score out of ten what level of fulfilment each activity gave you. Where the score is high there can be an inner glow which gives you the confidence that this is an activity you can build on.

Veronique was nervous when she first met a Cabinet Minister but soon found that she could relate to her easily. She was able to express her views clearly and recognise the political considerations that were influencing the Minister's decisions. Veronique got a buzz out of helping the Minister to crystallise her next steps.

Veronique recognised that she was getting a lot of fulfilment from working with Ministers. She volunteered to become a private secretary to a Minister. Her positive and decisive approach enabled the private office to run effectively, with the Minister being delighted with her contribution. This sense of fulfilment gave Veronique the confidence to see how she could further develop her career at senior levels within Government service.

In practice

- What activities give you the greatest levels of personal fulfilment now?

- How can you build on those activities and take your engagement with them to the next level?

- Are there some activities that give you fulfilment which if focused on too much can distort the way you want to balance your priorities?

- What is likely to give you most fulfilment in five years' time?

WHEN ARE YOU AT YOUR MOST EFFECTIVE?

KNOWING WHEN YOU ARE at your most effective provides an essential foundation for balancing priorities well in order to build longer-term success.

The idea

I am at my most effective in thinking through how to tackle a difficult issue when I travel on an early morning train to London. I am at my best in talking through complicated issues with others in the afternoon. Experience has taught me that my brain is at its most reflective and creative thinking alone in the morning, and better in dialogue with others in the afternoon. Normally the requirements of the working day do not mesh with these preferences, hence I have taught myself to operate in different ways at different times of day. But knowing my preferences allows me to allocate the most effective moments for hard thinking or difficult conversations.

It can be helpful to reflect in your current role on what are the tasks that are most important to your boss, your colleagues and your sponsors. Those tasks then need to be allocated to moments when you are in your most productive frame of mind, so you can deliver on them effectively. It is helpful to ask yourself what longer-term issues require you to be at your most effective, and then to allocate times when you can bring appropriate levels of intellectual energy to deal with those issues.

The corollary is that when you are not feeling effective in dealing with an issue it is normally best to park that issue, even for a short while, and return to it when you can approach it with a more engaged and positive mind-set.

Veronique knew that she was at her most effective if she could chunk up the day and the week into different activities. She dealt with e-mails in half-hour blocks. She carved out time to meet with key people in the Department for 20-minute catch-up conversations on a regular basis. She allocated difficult issues she needed to think through to a two-hour block on a Tuesday morning when she went to another part of the building to work. Veronique agreed with her Minister the times when she would be available to her and when she would be committed on other activities within the Department.

In practice

- What are the key areas where you need to be most effective in your work?

- How best do you allocate your time and energy so that they are focused on those areas where the expectations on you are highest?

- How best do you control the use of your time and energy so that you are at your most effective on the most important issues?

- What practical steps can you now take to balance your priorities so you work with the grain of your preferences?

WHAT HELPS YOU BALANCE YOUR PRIORITIES?

BEING CLEAR what and who helps you balance your priorities can provide a secure framework for making decisions.

The idea

We may sometimes wonder how we arrive at our judgements as to how we balance priorities at work with our family and community commitments. But there is often an underlying set of explanations about our instinctive decisions that are deep within us. It can be worth asking yourself why you tend to balance priorities in a particular way and how fixed that formula is. The underlying explanation might be that our automatic way of balancing priorities comes from our childhood or a particularly influential phase of life.

Ask yourself which priority you should tackle first that would best unblock other priorities or reduce the inner guilt that flows from putting things off for too long.

It can be helpful to distinguish between short-term and longer-term priorities. What do you need to invest time in to help build your credibility or expertise in a way that will best equip you to reach the type of goal that is most important to you in the longer term?

Think about who can enable you to balance your priorities. Ideally we each need trusted others with whom we can talk about priorities, who have our best interests at heart, and who are not preoccupied with their own wellbeing or interests. A wise mentor or trusted friend can be a valuable sounding-board as we talk through how our different priorities fit together.

Veronique trusted the perspectives of her brother and a contemporary at work. When she had difficult decisions about which post to apply for or how to use her time to best effect, Veronique would always talk to these two individuals. Their perspectives were not always identical, but always gave her valuable insights. Increasingly Veronique began to talk to her boyfriend, Ben, about priorities, but interestingly, he was never the first person she talked to as she did not think his views were completely dispassionate given the growing emotional link between them.

In practice

- What is your default way of balancing priorities and where do you think that originates from?

- How do you distinguish between short-term and long-term priorities?

- Who gives you the best advice about how you balance priorities? Can you talk to them more?

- When might emotional factors mean that the perspective of a mentor or good friend is not as dispassionate as you would like?

WHAT CAN DERAIL YOUR PRIORITIES?

KNOWING WHAT FORCES have the ability to derail our priorities gives us valuable insight into how to stay on course for success.

The idea

We may feel that we are maintaining a reasonable balance between our commitments to a longer-term career, our effectiveness in the day job, our family and our involvement in the local community. But we may be operating with no spare capacity.

If someone at home is ill our initial reaction is to work harder to get everything else done, when realism requires us to reduce our time commitment to some activities. Perhaps we have to take a break from some community activities. Perhaps we need to reduce the amount of time we give to particular work activities or delegate more to others. These steps require a conscious decision to stop doing certain things or to invest less time in certain activities. We might think that what is derailing us is a health issue in the family when in reality what is derailing us is an over-conscientious approach, with our pride getting in the way.

Sometimes our priorities do need to be derailed. We can become fixated on a particular set of priorities and not adjust them in the light of changes in circumstances. Perhaps when we are recovering from being ill or at the end of a holiday, that can be a good moment to review the way our priorities sit alongside each other and decide which ones can now be dispensed with and which should take greater prominence.

Sometimes when our priorities are derailed our confidence is knocked. Often when we feel derailed the reasons are entirely outside our control. What matters is recognising that we have been caught by unexpected events which were not of our making.

Veronique enjoyed working as principal private secretary to her Minister. When this Minister was reshuffled a new Minister was appointed who wanted to bring her own private secretary with her. Veronique therefore found herself instantly without a post. She oscillated between being angry and distraught. She felt it entirely unfair that she was being removed from this post by a new Minister who did not know her. Veronique felt her career was being derailed.

It took the wise counsel of a colleague a few years older to help Veronique recognise that these things happen and that she needed to move forward and not feel resentful. Veronique was quickly appointed to another post, leading on a new piece of policy work. Her time as a private secretary had built her credibility, which ensured she was sought after for other demanding jobs.

In practice

- Be conscious about what might derail your priorities

- Accept that someone else derailing your priorities might be exactly what is needed

- Believe that good can come out of any situation, even when your initial feeling is that you have been derailed

HOW SHOULD YOUR PRIORITIES BE CHANGING NOW?

OUR PRIORITIES NEED TO keep evolving in the light of changing personal preferences and external circumstances.

The idea

As the children in our lives grow older how we spend time with them changes. The priority when they are small is to keep them warm and safe. As they grow older the priority is to help them develop and learn. In their teenage years the priority might be to keep up with them as they become physically fitter than us. The priorities keep changing over time.

Our priorities in terms of building success in our work similarly change over time. In some periods maximising our financial income is the most important consideration. In other phases creating enough time to influence projects that are most significant to us is a top priority. In another phase what is particularly important is how we develop and grow the capability of people we are working with.

It can be helpful to do a stock-take at least once a year, thinking through what are your longer-term aspirations and what priorities need to be followed to help you reach those aspirations. In my coaching work I often ask people to think about the type of role they would like to fill in five or ten years' time and then invite them to reflect on what might be their priorities over the next year to give them a reasonable prospect of delivering on these aspirations.

Veronique aspired to being a Director in a Government Department by the time she was 40. She began to think through with a coach what capabilities and experience she needed to build up in order for this aspiration to be realisable. She recognised that there needed to be some individual successes which were attributable to her, alongside clear evidence that she built effective teams and contributed effectively to initiatives across the whole organisation. Veronique recognised that she needed to prioritise developing her impact and reputation within her part of the organisation and corporately across both the Department and the Government.

In practice

- How best do you set aside time to review your longer-term priorities?

- To what extent have your longer-term priorities become ossified?

- What new priorities is it time to crystallise and what existing priorities is it time to drop?

HOW DO YOU PREPARE FOR FUTURE PRIORITIES?

WE CAN BE SO focused on our current priorities that we do not think through future priorities.

The idea

Our current priority might be our postgraduate degree, our latest project, getting a promotion, or an all-consuming personal relationship. It is not always easy to think ahead to anticipate future priorities. When we are consumed in an interesting job we may not give much thought to our continued professional development. It is when we are immersed in an interesting role that we can potentially get maximum benefit from a focused university course or even an MBA.

The individual who leads a sports team, or becomes a school governor, or takes on a leadership role in a church, is both making a valuable current contribution and developing capabilities and experience which can be relevant for future priorities involving leading activities at work or in a voluntary capacity.

It is always worth asking yourself what might your future priorities be and how you can best prepare for such possibilities. This might be about investing in skills, or it could be about building up a network of supporters or colleagues with whom you can talk through ideas and future possibilities.

One of the biggest changes in priorities comes with having children. Farsighted people in their twenties start building a range of skills and experiences as they have available time and energy, recognising that time will be in shorter supply when children need to be looked after.

Veronique recognised that she had a strong internal desire to be a parent. She was deliberately aiming to take on different roles in her twenties and reach a particular level within Government before starting a family. Veronique recognised that there was no guarantee about becoming pregnant at a time of her choosing, but she was increasingly thinking that a partnership with Ben could work well over the longer term. She recognised there were a lot of future uncertainties, but was deliberate about the roles she applied for and the type of contribution she sought to make within the Department and in her local community.

In practice

- Review, on a periodic basis, what your future priorities might be

- Look at your priorities across the whole of your life, recognising that some priorities are your choice and some will be a consequence of events outside your control (e.g. the declining health of parents)

- Plan deliberately how you commit time and energy to preparing for future potential priorities

- Recognise that future priorities might end up looking very different from how they appear at the moment

HOW READY ARE YOU TO RESPOND TO THE CHANGING PRIORITIES OF OTHERS?

IT IS IMPORTANT NOT to take for granted the priorities of those closest to us.

The idea

A boss to whom you feel committed decides to move to another job. Your partner suddenly decides that they want to work part-time, or they apply for a job in another part of the country. Our first reaction can be to feel let down, with our views not having been taken properly into account. But there is no reason why our boss should be influenced by our preferences. There is equally no reason why we should control the choices made by our spouse or partner.

As we seek to make decisions about our longer-term priorities we are always subject to the effects of a myriad of decisions by others. The promotion policy of your organisation might change. Jobs might be relocated to another part of the world. The effect of economic change might be to increase your opportunities or drastically reduce them.

We are for ever living with the consequences of decisions by others. Sometimes we can anticipate the changing priorities, but often our influence is tangential or non-existent.

Within the family unit it is always worth seeking to explore how priorities might be changing and whether the aspirations that are most important to you can be kept open or are best placed in the 'very unlikely to happen' box. As priorities change for those closest to us it is important to be able to adapt so that we are not living with long-term disappointments that can damage our future wellbeing.

Veronique was surprised when her boyfriend, Ben, announced that he was going to leave his current role and work for an international organisation which would require him initially to be based in Geneva. Veronique had begun to build an image in her mind of a long-term partnership, but this type of geographic separation had not been on her agenda.

Veronique took some time to adjust to Ben's new work aspiration. She was equally ambitious but did not want to move from the Department where she worked. She began to accept that the relationship with Ben was perhaps not the long-term partnership she had hoped for.

In practice

- Accept that there will be moments when you will be taken by surprise by the changing priorities of others

- Accept with equanimity when changing priorities mean that work or personal partnerships may not last for as long as you hoped

- When the priorities of others change, recognise that you may have to work through an emotional reaction first before you can focus on the future

HOW DO YOU RECOVER FROM MISJUDGED PRIORITIES?

WE NEED TIME and good conversations in order to recover and move on from misjudged priorities.

The idea

Sometimes life can feel like being at a horseracing event where we have 'backed the wrong horse'. I vividly remember two occasions when I supported a leader who then fell out of favour. I was typecast as a supporter of the wrong individual. I had made what others regarded as misjudgements, which in one case was career-limiting.

As we seek to build our success we need to recognise that we will periodically be recovering from misjudged priorities. There is an unavoidable inevitability about this which we need to come to terms with.

Sometimes we will invest in people who move on or let us down. On other occasions we might invest a lot of time and energy in a project which fails. On other occasions we may be spending time developing a skill which turns out to be of limited application.

One perspective to bring might be that every year will include two or three instances of misjudged priorities. If we can accept this inevitability, and the learning which will result from misjudging priorities, then we can move on without feeling personally damaged by these experiences.

When you have misjudged a priority it can help to write down what you have learnt and how best you can move on. When you recognise that you have misjudged a priority in one area of life it can help to reflect on priorities that have turned out well in other areas of life.

Veronique felt that at her low moments she had misjudged the priority she attached to building a relationship with Ben. She thought sometimes that she had misjudged the way she had led her project team and tried to do too much of the work herself and not thought enough about longer-term priorities. Veronique took careful stock with a good friend about her learning from situations when she felt her priorities had not been as thought out as they should have been. Veronique was now clearer about how she was going to balance her personal and professional aspirations and priorities in the future.

In practice

- How have you recovered from misjudged priorities in the past?

- What currently feels like a misjudged priority which you need to recognise and move on from?

- How do you learn from misjudging the balancing of different priorities across family, community and work?

- What attitudes do you want to put in place so as to reduce the risk of misjudged priorities leading to long-term frustration?

SECTION B
UNDERSTAND THE DRIVERS OF YOUR AMBITION

FAMILY INFLUENCES

WE ARE OUR PARENTS' CHILDREN whether we like it or not. The attitudes we inherit and pick up from our parents are central to the way we view success.

The idea

From an early age expectations are built into us about what is success. For the baby success is about waking up and going to sleep at the right time. For the toddler success is about eating their food, following instructions, and playing with toys without destroying them. For the youngster going to school, success is about dressing on their own, being co-operative with other children and being willing to listen and learn.

Our parents reinforce these definitions of success through the way they encourage and reward behaviour. They set aspirations and shape desires. Through approval or disapproval they form within us a set of expectations about what constitutes success and how success is attained.

Grandparents can be just as influential as parents when a youngster spends extended time with them. Where there is deep affection for a grandparent, their values and approaches can become strongly embedded.

To understand the drivers of our ambition, we can look to our parents. Often we will mirror their approaches. Sometimes, following difficult experiences in our childhood and teenage years, we may have reacted strongly against their influence and now exhibit a set of attitudes to success which are contrary to those of our parents.

When I am coaching individuals I might ask questions like, 'What elements of your mother or father's personality continue to live on in you?' or, 'What might others observe in you which is similar to your parents in your attitude to success?'

Helen's father worked in a munitions factory as a technician. He had left school aged 16 and studied for qualifications at evening class. He was disciplined and effective in his job, without ever aspiring to become a manager. Helen's mother worked in a shop and enjoyed the buzz of talking with customers.

Helen's parents provided a secure home for her to grow up in. They wanted Helen to have opportunities for education, which they never had. They were ambitious for her throughout her school days and praised her academic success. They reinforced in her the importance of working co-operatively with other pupils and her teachers. They taught her to be single-minded without being rebellious.

In practice

- How strongly do your parents' attitudes feed through into your perspective about what is success?

- To what extent do the attributes of your mother or father continue to live on in you?

- How have other significant family members influenced the nature of your aspirations?

- In what ways are your beliefs about ambition and success entirely different from those of your parents and why is this?

12 CULTURAL EXPECTATIONS

CULTURAL EXPECTATIONS CAN SHAPE our ideas of what are approved and disapproved behaviours and can create both expectations and inhibitions.

The idea

The attitudes of the community in which we grew up will have rubbed off on us. As a youngster we will have sensed what behaviours are approved or disapproved of. As a child our tendency will have been to exhibit behaviours that result in approval. In our teenage years we are likely to have exhibited a wider mix of behaviours, some of which won approval whereas others we may have deliberately chosen because they were contrary to the normal expectations of the community in which we grew up.

If we went to university our expectations will have been shaped by our interactions with fellow students and staff. Our eyes may have been opened to wider opportunities, with success taking on a very different character. At school success was about examination results or performance on the sports field. At university success may become linked more to what you would do after higher education.

In your twenties the influence of your peer group can be significant. We may be asking ourselves searching questions, such as, in which direction have different friends set off and what is the progress they are making? What avenues are individuals exploring that catch my imagination? What different types of opportunities can I see myself exploring before setting up a permanent home?

We are shaped by a sequence of cultural expectations resulting from our community background, our educational experience, and our friends and colleagues. It is worth identifying what type of influence each group has had on our attitude to success.

Helen had been a diligent schoolgirl who focused on getting good examination results. The cultural expectation in her school was about working hard and being compliant. Helen felt a new liberation at university meeting people from varied backgrounds. The mix of values and behaviours was both a shock and an inspiration. She was entering a world where success had many different definitions. Her friends, post-university, were all ambitious in different ways. She became hungry to share in some of their success, without fully understanding what for her would be success.

In practice

- How strongly has the local community in which you grew up shaped your attitudes about what are approved or disapproved behaviours?

- In what ways did your school experience help shape a sense of ambition in you?

- At what point did you move from an inherited view about what success is to a more personal view of what matters most for you?

- What has liberated you from the cultural expectations others might have placed on you about what is success?

THE DESIRE TO MAKE A DIFFERENCE

13

THE DESIRE TO MAKE a difference can be deeply embedded in us. It is worth understanding where that desire comes from and how it is best expressed.

The idea

Many of us feel a desire to make a difference, but it is often difficult to explain where this desire comes from. It can result from the influence of parents, our community, or our cultural background. Often the desire to make a difference results from interaction with key people in our lives, such as a teacher who inspired us in a particular academic subject or topic. Or it might have been a sports coach who drew out from us qualities of resolve and determination.

We might have engaged during our later teenage years in voluntary community activity and observed pain or dysfunction in families or communities. Such experience might have inspired us to think through how to help others to address current difficulties and not be captive to them.

We might have seen a film about poverty or family brutality and been shocked at a reality very different from our own. Out of this disturbance to our relatively cosy world might have arisen a desire to enable others to make a difference to their lives.

We are likely to have been making compromises between the lifestyle we want to adopt and the ways we want to help make a difference to the lives of other people. We might have explored making a difference through becoming a member of a caring profession, or by marketing goods and providing services that give people greater freedom to choose how they are going to use their time and talents well.

Helen was conscious when at university that there was a tension between her compliant focusing on building a traditional pathway to success, and the attraction of being rebellious by doing something radically different to her parents. Part of her wanted to make a difference towards solving world poverty by working as a volunteer in Africa. Another part of her saw the role of politics as crucial and wanted to go down a political activist route. Another part of her wanted to start a family and influence the next generation through being a good parent.

Helen recognised there was a complex set of emotions going on in her. She recognised that this desire to make a difference would always be part of her but its expression might well change over time.

In practice

- Where did you want to make a difference in your teenage years and how much is that still part of you?

- Who have been the particularly influential people who helped shape your views about what it means to make a difference?

- What tensions have you felt within yourself about different spheres in which you want to make a difference?

- What is the current internal debate within you about where you want to make a difference, and how strongly held are each of those competing perspectives?

14 THE FINANCIAL INCENTIVE

BEING HONEST ABOUT financial priorities is important in shaping how you take forward your aspirations for the future.

The idea

Rhetoric and reality can sometimes be at odds when we think about what happens to us financially. We might say that we do not care about the level of income we receive, and yet we have a series of expectations about our lifestyle. If we like eating out, drinking wine or going on holidays, these luxuries have to be paid for.

The need for financial security can be deeply embedded within us, leading us to want to accumulate savings and investments for a rainy day. Such a desire for financial independence is commendable but can be constraining if financial wellbeing becomes an overriding objective.

Separating emotions from financial preferences is not necessarily straightforward. We can either have fixed ideas about what is financial security or be excessively blasé and expect the future to look after itself. Perhaps the appropriate approach is to look dispassionately at what financial provision will be compatible with what you want to do with your life. This can help build realism about the constraints you want to put on yourself and the freedoms you want to have.

A preoccupation with events in the future can be disabling to what you do in the present. But a disregard of finance for the future will be debilitating if there is no forward provision for times when income is tight.

There was never much spare money in Helen's family home. Her mother spent the weekly income carefully and saved up for an annual family holiday by the seaside. There was a bottle of sherry at Christmas, but little else by way of luxury. Helen was grateful for the financial discipline her parents taught her. She did not waste money but she also acknowledged that she could be ultra-cautious in her use of finances.

Helen trained herself to recognise the importance of investing money in books, having meals with interesting people and going to historic places on holiday. She recognised that she would need a serious income stream to provide the future security she wanted, but she was able to sit lightly to the financial ambitions that seemed so important to some of her peers from university. She did not need to live in a big mansion, but she wanted the security and privacy of her own home.

In practice

- What is the minimum income you need to provide the lifestyle that is important to you?

- How deeply embedded within you is the financial incentive and to what extent does it distort your attitudes and behaviour?

- When might your financial desires get out of proportion in terms of shaping what matters most to you?

- What type of financial income would give you the freedom to take forward the mix of activities that are most important to you?

- How important is it to you to be able to give away a significant amount of your income?

15 THE NEED FOR CONTROL

BE HONEST WITH YOURSELF about what is your need for control.

The idea

The desire for control is deeply embedded within us. It is worth being honest with yourself about what you want to control and where you are content to be controlled or strongly influenced by others. We may say we want to be in control of our future but do not need to be in control of each individual activity, or we might be in danger of wanting to control everything we are involved in.

Being part of a sports team is an excellent antidote to the desire to control everything going on around you. To be an effective team member, you are controlling your own contribution, and contributing to but not controlling the whole endeavour. As soon as one player tries to control other team members they are likely to be ignored, ridiculed or dropped. Those with a strong desire to control have often learnt skills of influencing others without overtly controlling them.

The need for control has clear benefits. It leads you to want to manage your career and to be deliberate about the activities you are involved in and the relationships you establish. The desire for control can then be expressed by influencing the way decisions are reached, and not about directly having your own way.

Having no desire to control can be dangerous if the result is that you are pushed around by the preferences of others. That is fine if it is a deliberate choice. Perhaps in a family setting control moves from one person to another on different subjects, by explicit or tacit agreement.

When I coach individuals I often ask them, 'What is it you can control and what can you not control, and how do you keep a clear distinction between these two things?' My objective is to enable someone to differentiate objectively and not to have false illusions about the level of control they do have.

Helen wanted to be in control of her own destiny. She liked her independence and wanted a career. She did not seek a spouse, partially because she did not want to be at risk of being controlled by anyone else. She had read history at university and did a law conversion course. She aspired to being a barrister so she could be in control of the arguments she was deploying and be responsible for her own career.

As Helen progressed as a barrister she recognised that her control was limited. She was dependent upon the evidence she was given, the views of the witnesses, the approach of the other advocates and the attitude of the Judge. The clerk at her Chambers seemed to control her life in terms of the cases she was given, but she still controlled how she presented her case in court and how she spent the rest of her time.

In practice

- When do you need to be in control and when are you happy to be controlled by others?

- How readily are you able to translate that need for control into an ability to influence?

- When has a desire to control been damaging in isolating you?

- How have you used the desire to control in a focused way, enabling others to control what they can do best?

16 THE EXAMPLE OF ROLE MODELS

ROLE MODELS HAVE A powerful influence upon us in shaping our expectations about appropriate ambition and achievable outcomes.

The idea

All of us have role models who have significantly influenced us at different points in our lives. Gerald Blake was a Geography Professor who interviewed me as a potential undergraduate at Durham University when I was 18, and later pointed me in the direction of Regent College in Vancouver when I was 21. As a professor he always brought a thoughtful and purposeful approach, encouraging me to think constructively about the type of career I might embark upon. When I received an Honorary Doctorate from Durham University recently, 45 years after graduating with a bachelor's degree, I was able to thank Gerald Blake for the way he had helped shape my thinking and next steps nearly five decades earlier. It has been a delight to dedicate this book to him.

As a coach I might say to someone, 'Who are the five key people who have most shaped your aspirations at different stages in your life?' I encourage my coachee to identify the attitudes and behaviours of these role models which have become embedded in their own beliefs.

It is important not to be too constrained by role models. It is worth remembering that they have feet of clay and reflecting on how you differentiate yourself from them. I might ask a coachee, 'What three things from a role model are most embedded in you?' and, 'What is one thing a role model does that you deliberately choose not to do?'

Helen greatly admired a senior barrister in her Chambers. He was bright, quick-witted and could handle a brief well. Helen admired his discipline in mastering a case and his ability to identify key issues and put his points across succinctly. She learnt a huge amount through acting as his junior on a number of big cases. Working with this senior barrister helped build her confidence and her repertoire of ways of putting complicated points across.

However, there was sometimes a touch of arrogance in this barrister's approach and under stress he could over-emphasise points. Helen recognised when this was about to happen and told herself that she would know when to stop and not become over-emotional in the way her colleague was sometimes inclined to do.

In practice

- Acknowledge what you have learnt from role models and remember to tell them what you most appreciate about how they have inspired you

- Be dispassionate in reflecting on what you have embedded in your approach from role models and how much you have embraced their practices into your repertoire

- Be frank with yourself about what aspects of a role model's approach you are deliberately not adopting

- Recognise that others may be regarding you as their role model

THE RELEVANCE OF A FAITH PERSPECTIVE

17

OFTEN A FAITH PERSPECTIVE brings a strong focus on the overriding values and behaviours underpinning our reactions to new situations.

The idea

A faith perspective will always provide a lens through which issues are considered and choices made. Someone from a Hindu background will normally have a strong focus on compassion and mindfulness of others. An individual from a Jewish background will bring a strong sense of community and history. Someone from a Muslim background is likely to bring a focus on journey, regularity and self-sacrifice. Someone from a Christian background is likely to bring a strong sense of service, and of using talents and gifts to best effect.

Someone's faith perspective may be built deep within them because of their family or community heritage. Sometimes we do not fully appreciate how our instinctive reactions have been conditioned by the faith perspective of our parents or the predominant faith of the community in which we grew up.

Our faith perspective might be both inherited and deliberately cultivated. We may be adopting practices we respect in a number of religious traditions or we may be embracing wholeheartedly one particular faith perspective and worldview.

Building success across our lives depends on integrating the faith perspective we have with the rest of our life priorities. If we keep faith, work and family in entirely different boxes there is likely to be a discontinuity, with one part of our lives rubbing up against another.

Our personal wholeness depends on allowing our faith perspective to influence the way we live the rest of our lives, and allowing the pragmatic experience of work and life to inform the way we interpret and live out our faith perspective.

Helen grew up in a committed Catholic family. The result was a strong sense of serving others, a need for humility, and strong moral values, drive and determination, coupled with a sense of guilt if she did not live up to the standards she had set herself or if she made mistakes.

Helen recognised that she was an exemplar of both Catholic determination and independence, and Catholic guilt. She fully understood the strengths and liabilities that came from being part of the Catholic tradition, and was able to smile to herself at these different reactions.

In practice

- What have you inherited from the faith perspective of your parents or your home community?

- Is there a faith perspective embedded within you and how does that influence the way you react in different situations?

- How much do you explicitly own a particular faith perspective and allow that to influence your attitudes to work and life more generally?

- How aligned are your perspectives and behaviours between your faith principles and your pragmatism at work?

YOUR EXPECTATIONS AND THOSE OF OTHERS

SETTING CLEAR EXPECTATIONS can enable us or constrain us. The expectations of others can liberate us or box us in.

The idea

Creating clear expectations about what we are able to achieve can be helpful in engendering a strong sense of ambition and motivation. The teenager who builds an expectation that they can be an excellent police officer is likely to be motivated enough to go through the selection processes with a reasonable chance of success, but an expectation that they will become the Chief Constable is almost inevitably going to lead to disappointment.

The dilemma is, how do you create expectations that have a positive effect on both learning and motivation, without being so tied to a specific expectation that you become racked with disappointment if you do not reach the desired outcome? The balance needed is to combine a clear ambition with sitting lightly to that aspiration. Progress comes through recognising that it is helpful to be building up a set of experiences that will equip you to hold a responsible post, without being wedded to one particular type of senior leadership role.

The expectations of others can be helpful or destructive. A positive expectation from a colleague or boss can give us confidence and motivation to succeed in a particular endeavour. It can build self-belief about what is possible and how best we reach a good outcome. But an expectation from a family member, colleague or boss that we believe is out of reach can leave us drained, dejected and sometimes devastated.

It is important to reflect carefully on the expectations of others. Are they realistic at a stretch, or are they unrealistic and more an expression of the other person's desires rather than a sensible assessment of what might be possible?

Helen had an inner desire to become a Judge. At times this ambition meant she drove herself hard as a barrister in taking on a wide range of different cases. The feedback she received from her professional colleagues was encouraging about this long-term possibility, but Helen knew she had to sit lightly to it and not assume that becoming a member of the judiciary would be an inevitable outcome of her hard work. She recognised that as a barrister she was using skills of analysis and argument that could be applicable in a range of different contexts. She would love to be a Judge but was not going to let that expectation, or the expectations of others, drive her every decision.

In practice

- Where do your expectations about yourself come from? Are you comfortable with them?

- Are you over-influenced by the expectations of others and can you sit lightly to them?

- How are your expectations about the next steps in your career and wider life influencing your current decisions? Are you happy about the way that is happening?

- What new expectation do you want to build into your planned assumptions about the future?

THE EFFECT OF YOUR OWN SELF-WORTH

Our view of our own self-worth can enable us to move into new spheres, or inhibit our freedom. There are always choices to be made.

The idea

How much do we value our own distinctive character and experiences? If we brand ourselves as unconfident, anxious, fickle and poor at making decisions, then we are likely to act in a way that is consistent with this perspective. We end up creating our own self-fulfilling prophecies of doom. If we feel a victim of circumstances we are likely to become a victim of circumstances. If we feel we have suffered as a result of decisions by others, with our confidence knocked, we may secretly quite like being able to blame others for our problems.

Self-worth is about recognising the reality of your situation and the extent to which you feel stuck, but it is also about thinking beyond the immediate emotions into what might be possible going forward. Self-worth is about recognising your strengths and believing the positive things that people say about you, and then seeking to apply those gifts in new situations.

Self-worth is not believing you can build your qualities and uniqueness in an unrealistic way. Self-worth comes from listening to the perspectives of a wide range of trusted others so that you reach a balanced view about where you can contribute most effectively and how your distinctive qualities can be developed further. Self-worth comes from recognising you are respected and loved by family and friends, warts and all.

Helen sometimes felt out of place in the court room. She had travelled a long way from the council house where she was brought up. She did not always believe that she had the capabilities to be a top-flight barrister. She needed to be receiving affirmation from her colleagues in order to recognise her own self-worth. When Helen had moments of self-doubt she knew who were the people she needed to talk to who would help her rebuild her self-esteem and reinforce in her the commitment to take on increasingly complex cases as a barrister. She recognised that her description of her frailties kept her human, and that she needed to hold on to the belief in her own self-worth in order to survive and thrive in a competitive world.

In practice

- How secure is your level of self-worth?

- What can make you anxious about your self-worth, and how best do you address that situation?

- How best do you hold together an honest assessment of your own frailties, alongside a firm belief in the need to exercise the gifts and qualities you have been given?

- Who are the significant others who can help you balance your understanding your frailties and building on your talents?

THE PLACE OF INNER COMPULSIVENESS

INNER COMPULSIVENESS IS BOTH a strength and a liability. How best do we direct and train our compulsiveness?

The idea

We recognise compulsiveness in others – which can be unattractive or endearing. We see some people who never stop talking and who intervene too much in meetings; their compulsiveness is off-putting and insensitive. We observe others who have a compulsive desire to assist others and enable them to succeed. Sometimes this form of compulsiveness is misplaced if it seeks to take away someone's discretion. On the other hand the compulsiveness of the teacher to enable all their pupils to read more effectively leads to a range of different practical approaches to help children develop their reading skills.

We all have a compulsive side. Sometimes it can tend to obsession or addiction, but recognising our compulsive side and then training it and steering it can be powerful. If someone has a compulsion to speak, how can they become a good public speaker? If someone has a compulsion towards forensic analysis, how can that be turned into an asset? If someone has a compulsion to get into the details, how can they work with others to bring a complementary set of approaches and skills?

There may be a compulsiveness to succeed in a particular career or a dream that keeps recurring. It is worth asking ourselves what is going on here. What is my inner psyche saying to me about what is most important? The inner drive to be a doctor or engineer may be an emotional, compulsive reaction caused by a myriad of factors. We may have a healthy compulsiveness about an end goal we want to reach, but we need to watch if that compulsiveness is so overriding that it becomes destructive to other priorities.

Helen recognised that a compulsiveness had grown in her to speak her mind. This had been hidden in childhood, liberated at university, and developed in her work as a barrister. This compulsiveness to speak her mind meant that she was not daunted by the arguments of other barristers. She recognised that it could be self-limiting if speaking her mind meant she annoyed too many people. She recognised that speaking her mind openly in a work context was different from saying what she thought with friends and family.

Helen appreciated that this capacity to speak her mind without fear or favour was an important quality that needed to be used wisely if she was to make the difference she wanted, both in individual court cases and in her profession more generally. She recognised that it was a major strength, but also a potential liability if she failed to be selective in how she deployed it.

In practice

- When does your inner compulsiveness get in the way of what is important to you?

- When is your inner compulsiveness a strength that enables you to break out from unhelpful constraints?

- How can you use your inner compulsiveness as a strength and positive quality rather than a liability?

SECTION C
ADDRESS WHAT MIGHT HOLD YOU BACK

LACK OF CONFIDENCE

THE MAIN INHIBITOR OF progress is a lack of confidence. Learning to be confident is crucial to moving forward.

The idea

Most of us are confident in one sphere and lack confidence in others. The question is, how do we transfer the confidence we experience in one situation into other contexts?

A young leader might feel inhibited at work and fully confident at home. How can the individual's qualities and confidence best transfer from the family environment, where they are uninhibited, into the work environment, where their confidence often melts away?

A lack of confidence can mean we come over as insensitive, hesitant and inept. Once we feel confident in a situation we get into a rhythm, our words flow, and we feel and look fully engaged.

We can build up our confidence through doing small things well. Once we have chaired a small meeting effectively our confidence grows to be able to chair bigger meetings. Once we have spoken at a seminar of 12 people we can become more confident about speaking at a conference with 60 people.

Confidence comes as we develop ways of preparing our content of what we say and our frame of mind. There may be routines that help our confidence, such as wearing a particular pair of shoes or ensuring we always arrive a few minutes early.

We can gradually overcome a lack of confidence through recognising our successes, transferring confidence from one sphere to another, and being clear about the impact we have had in the past and can have in the future. It can help to share our ideas openly with others, so that our confidence is not based purely on our own reflections but also draws on the reflections of others.

Aisha had been brought up in a caring Hindu home in which she was taught to serve others rather than take the lead herself. She had been a studious pupil and done an accountancy degree. She was effective in her work but tended to lack confidence. As a young trainee in the accountancy section of a national retail organisation she was given positive feedback about her work and encouragement to contribute more fully.

Aisha was aware that she did not come over as confident and knew that she needed to work on this. She was confident within her community, and deliberately put herself into situations where she was transferring her confidence from her community environment into the work context. Gradually she felt more at home making contributions.

In practice

- Recognise when you at your most confident and observe what enables you to be confident

- Recognise what triggers a sense of low confidence and how best you anticipate those triggers

- Think through how you might be bolder in taking ideas forward in situations where you feel your confidence is limited

- Give yourself a gold star when your confidence is at a higher level than you expected

22 INEXPERIENCE

INEXPERIENCE IS PERHAPS the easiest inhibitor to address. Overcoming it requires careful planning and the commitment of time.

The idea

Inexperience can be about a lack of knowledge or limited understanding about the way outcomes are delivered or people brought on board.

Sometimes what is holding us back is relatively easy to address. We need to understand more about a particular business area and how things get done in that sphere. This involves talking to a range of people and gradually building awareness, a factual understanding and a sensitivity of how decisions are made.

We may start off thinking that we have limited experience, but we might realise that we have transferable insights that enable us to assess a situation reasonably quickly and develop an appreciation about what we can contribute.

When you visit a new city you spend time building up knowledge about how its transport system works. You do not know the city but you bring knowledge of how other city transport systems operate. You may not have worked in a particular organisation before, but you will bring from previous experiences an understanding of how good organisations operate.

The fact that you do not have experience of a particular area of work or organisation can be a plus as much as a minus. You can bring a wider perspective and experience of how other organisations operate.

You will view the new organisation with fresh eyes. Your inexperience might be your prime asset and not your biggest liability.

When you start a new role it is important to be honest about your lack of experience and have a clear plan for filling in gaps of knowledge and insight. Then you can create a perfectly sensible platform on which to build your credibility.

Aisha knew that her two main gaps were knowledge of a particular accounting system and her inexperience in contributing to bigger meetings. She developed a plan for building her knowledge and experience in two these areas. She set aside time to develop her knowledge of the new accounting system.

Aisha offered to represent her group at a range of different meetings in order to practise contributing in environments which had previously felt alien to her. Being disciplined in addressing these areas of inexperience helped fill in her knowledge gaps and develop her confidence.

In practice

- See inexperience in some situations as an asset rather than a liability

- Be willing to bring a fresh pair of eyes in situations where you have limited experience

- Be honest about the gaps in your knowledge and experience and put together a plan to address those limitations

- See building capability as an on-going process for the rest of your life

FEELING YOU ARE AN IMPOSTOR

Sometimes you feel completely out of place and likely to be found out – but the feeling can pass as quickly as it arrives.

The idea

Most people suffer at some stage from the 'impostor syndrome'. All of a sudden you feel out of your depth or ill-equipped to cope with an unexpected situation.

You might have been confident one minute, but suddenly it feels as if your legs have given way beneath you, and you are struggling to find your voice. If feels as if you are fine one moment and breaking out in a cold sweat the next.

When the imposter syndrome strikes, you have to remind yourself that you are in a role on merit. Others believe in your credentials and experience, and do not see you as an impostor.

The sensation of feeling like an impostor can hit us at unexpected moments. When it does we may need to stand up and move around, or mentally talk firmly to the impostor, or thank the impostor for reminding us that we are a mixture of strengths and less robust characteristics.

Talking to others about their experience of being gripped by the imposter syndrome can help put this experience into perspective. Knowing how others have handled such attacks can give us confidence that this is not a terminal problem.

Aisha often felt out of place in a room of white, male, middleclass accountants. The risk was she slipped into a softer voice and hid in the corner. She needed to remind herself that she was in this office because others had recognised her experience and qualities. She had higher qualifications than many people in the room and had built a track record of successful pieces of work.

As Aisha's confidence grew the attacks of imposter syndrome became less frequent, but she was wary of being caught out. Sometimes she recognised the pattern of when she was likely to be caught out by the impostor syndrome. When she felt inadequate she stood up, walked around, looked outside the window and counted to ten. Then she put a smile back on her face and put the imposter syndrome back in its box.

In practice

- Draw from the experience of others about how they handle the imposter syndrome

- Recognise when you are likely to be in the grip of the imposter syndrome

- Practise techniques that move you into a different physical and emotional space so that the imposter syndrome is not able to grip you in a damaging way

- Say thank you to the imposter for helping to keep you humble

24 FEAR OF FAILURE

THE FEAR OF FAILURE can paralyse us and neutralise the best of intentions but it can also provide a valuable forewarning of risks.

The idea

A couple of years ago my eldest son convinced me to get into a kayak. I felt totally unstable and looked petrified because I was fearful of the kayak turning over. I held on to the paddle tightly as a means of balancing myself, but the fear of capsizing drained any desire to push out and paddle.

The fear of failure can hold us back from experimenting with using our gifts. We hold back from making a contribution in a meeting because people might think it is a silly point. We do not volunteer to chair a meeting because others might regard our way of chairing as poor. We are reluctant to take the lead on a project because we will be mortified if it does not succeed.

It can be worth befriending our fears. A fear might be a forewarning of a risk that it is right to address. When we are fearful we take careful steps and are wary of what might go wrong. A fear that becomes a cautious wariness can be helpful. A fear that grips us and stops us from acting is destructive.

A fear of failure can mean we freeze and are unable to act or make any decision. Addressing this type of fear involves understanding where it comes from, recognising how we have handled it effectively in the past, testing out the fear to see what substance it contains, talking through the fear with trusted others, and then taking some steps to demonstrate that the fear is unfounded. It helps to believe that it is possible to chair the next meeting of a committee without the world coming to an end. It can help if we accept that others are likely to appreciate our contribution, even if we start off feeling apprehensive about their likely reaction.

Aisha recognised that if she looked too much at one imposing person in a meeting then she could be gripped by fear of failure. She trained herself not to be preoccupied with that person and to be willing to look at all the people in the room, including those who encouraged her. Aisha tried to understand her fear of failure and tackle it in small steps, always logging the steps she took. Gradually she felt she was making progress, although it often felt like three steps forward, two steps back.

In practice

- Recall the times you felt a fear of failure in the past and how you reacted to it

- Tackle each fear a step at a time and log the progress you are able to make

- Accept that fears are often helpful in forewarning us of risks and difficulties

- If a particular person or situation prompts a fear of failure either avoid that person or situation, or limit your exposure to them, or prepare carefully

INHIBITIONS

INHIBITIONS COME IN MANY DIFFERENT SHAPES. It is worth understanding what are the inhibitions that affect us and how best we can address them.

The idea

You may feel inhibited about standing in front of someone who looks like your father or a former boss. If certain people are taking part in a meeting you can feel inhibited about expressing your view until you have heard what these people think. If you suspect that your comments might not be approved of by an influential person you might feel inhibited about expressing your view.

Your inhibitions might be deeply embedded within you and masquerade as values. Deference to people older than you may be a value in your cultural background, but we can end up using that value as an excuse for not contributing authoritatively in a meeting.

There can be deep-seated inhibitions because of where we come from, the way we speak, the way we look, or a minor physical disability. I am slightly hard of hearing and feel inhibited if I cannot hear a full conversation, hence the desire to sit in the middle of a meeting and not at its edges.

We may be inhibited about expressing clear views on paper because they might not be 100% right and might be questioned by others. Whatever our inhibitions, what matters is recognising them, being honest about their implications, practising moving on from those inhibitions and seeking to overcome them step by step.

Sometimes our inhibitions are a good thing. An inhibition that stops you getting into the details can be helpful if the contribution you need to bring comes from your wide experience and through bringing a different perspective. Hence the importance of asking yourself the question whether an inhibition is getting in the way, or is helping you keep your contribution at the right level.

Aisha was brought up in a culture where the boss was always treated with huge respect, and you did not question the judgements of your boss. She recognised that excessive deference to her boss was getting in the way of her doing her job well. She spoke openly with her boss about the cultural perspective she brought. Her boss was very understanding and from then on always encouraged Aisha to be direct with him and to express contrary views if she disagreed with him. He created an atmosphere which encouraged her to speak up more. As a consequence Aisha felt liberated by this new, more open working relationship and was for ever grateful to this individual for liberating her from her previous restraining perspective.

In practice

- Observe the link between your cultural background and your inhibitions

- Be honest with yourself and trusted colleagues about your inhibitions

- Address your inhibitions one at a time and practise doing tasks that you find uncomfortable

- Beware if you describe an inhibition as a personal value and recognise when this is a rationalisation

GLUE

YOU MAY BE THE GLUE holding an organisation together whom others appreciate and do not want to lose.

The idea

I was a member of a highly effective executive team for a number of years. When we had a subsequent reunion the chief executive described me as the glue that helped keep the team together. I had sought to build good-quality working relationships with each member of the team and always had good bilateral understandings with colleagues. To be described as the glue was for me a positive affirmation about what I had been trying to contribute to the team. It also helped that I was the Finance Director.

I have seen situations where someone is so important to a team in helping to glue it together that the other members assume the team cannot exist without that individual. The person is at risk of becoming stuck. The team members do not want them to move on and might even stand in the way of them moving to a different post.

If you are seen as crucial to a team, a perceived risk of collapse, if you leave, can hold you back. Your presence in a team might have become more important than your personal development or advancement.

It is a positive if other people want you in the team. It is a negative if they become over-dependent upon you and do not want you to leave when the time is right to do so. If you observe over-dependency happening it can be helpful to reach agreement about the timing or circumstances when you can move on. Perhaps it is a commitment to let you go after four months or when a particular job opportunity becomes available.

Aisha was delighted to be seen as an essential part of the property team, which took up 50% of her time. The role had helped build her confidence and enabled her to be less afraid of failure. She liked the way the team members sought her advice but she became apprehensive that they might be too dependent on her.

Team members wanted nothing to do with the finance figures and saw that as entirely for Aisha to handle. She welcomed the belief in her capabilities but was concerned that they were distancing themselves from the figures. She felt in danger of being trapped into this role for longer than was good for her because others were so dependent upon her. Although initially reluctant, the team leader agreed it would be right for Aisha to move on at the end of the financial year.

In practice

- Observe who provides the glue in different teams

- Recognise the value of being seen as the glue holding a team together

- Allow yourself to be the glue through building quality working relationships with different members of the team

- Beware if being the glue means a risk that the team believes it cannot thrive without you

INERTIA

INERTIA IS FINE in moderation but dangerous in excess.

The idea

Inertia can be helpful. There are times when it is right to do nothing. We can have a mental picture that success involves perpetual motion. But sometimes the result of perpetual motion is exhaustion.

There are moments when we need to stop, observe what is going on around us, take stock about our journey so far and reflect on next steps. On these occasions inertia is helpful. We need to slow down and stand still.

The opposite risk is that we enjoy inertia too much. We are feeling comfortable and content where we are. The world is not collapsing around us, we are reasonably happy and not feeling too stressed. We are not looking particularly to the future, allowing it to take care of itself.

This type of inertia can veer into complacency and self-satisfaction. Peering into the future can be unsettling, but can also forewarn us that the world is changing around us and we need to be more alert to those changes. It can be worth asking yourself the extent to which you are in the grip of inertia. Are you over-comfortable in your current role? Is there a risk of lapsing into complacency?

Inertia can happen for the best of reasons. For example, domestic pressures mean it is right not to be forcing the pace at work. But it is worth observing if we might be rationalising the situation and giving ourselves reasons that are more excuses than rational explanations.

When you are recovering from an operation pacing yourself gently is essential. But recovery reaches a point when too much inertia inhibits the next steps of the recovery.

Aisha enjoyed analysing figures. Being on top of the data gave her a sense of personal self-worth and enabled her to reassure herself that she was making a valuable contribution. She recognised that she needed to spend more time interpreting the figures and using that interpretation to challenge some of the company's assumptions. Entering that territory could be a bit threatening.

It was easier and more comfortable for Aisha to be doing the analysis of the figures than exploring the consequences of the interpretations for the future health of the organisation. Aisha recognised that if her career was to progress she needed to step out of her comfort zone, shake off her inertia, and be willing to be more assertive in setting out potentially unsettling implications.

In practice

- To what extent are you gripped by inertia?

- What elements of your inertia are entirely appropriate at this point because of the need to look after yourself or because of future uncertainties?

- What best enables you to move on from inertia?

- Who will help you recognise whether you are being complacent?

28 FRUSTRATION

FRUSTRATION CAN BE A CATALYST for action or it can destroy our resolve.

The idea

Frustration is a powerful agent for good. When we feel frustrated we are much more likely to take action. Frustration can lead to a resolve to change what is annoying us. When we feel emotionally frustrated it can alert us to areas where inertia has held us back. We can feel frustrated by an event or attitude all of a sudden, which helps us recognise that now is the moment to make a decision.

On the other hand we can get enmeshed in our own frustrations. If we think someone has let us down, or that events have gone against our interests, we can allow our frustrations to get a grip of us. When frustration leads to excessive annoyance, our emotions can be drained and leave us in a spiral of discontent.

It can be worth listing out your current frustrations and seeing which of them you can use to good effect, and which are potentially insidious and dangerous. When a frustration is having a negative effect it is worth putting energy into examining how that frustration can be understood, reduced or removed. It is only when we face up directly to the negative effects of frustration that we might find the resolve to do something about that frustration so we are not completely enmeshed within it.

If we find ourselves permanently annoyed with a colleague and frustrated by their behaviour this frustration can lead to dangerous distortions in what we do and how we relate to others. This might be the moment to have an honest conversation with that individual about the issue that is bugging you, or sharing openly some of your frustrations in a reflective way. Alternatively you might decide you are going to spend as little time as possible with the individual who frustrates you, until the annoyance begins to dissipate.

Aisha was frustrated by the dismissive way in which she was treated by a couple of the general managers, who seemed to either ignore her or be very critical about what she was doing. Her frustration was in danger of showing itself to others. It was certainly inhibiting her from being at her best.

Aisha sought to limit the way this frustration affected her contribution and mood. She told herself that she could be frustrated for five minutes each day, but no more. She tried to be cheerful in the company of the two general managers. She talked with others about whether they felt a similar level of frustration. When there was a 360° feedback exercise that included the general managers Aisha thought hard about what she wrote in the feedback. She made some carefully worded contributions that were direct while acknowledging the pressure the general managers were under.

In practice

- Remember how you have used frustration to good effect to prompt constructive change to take place

- See frustration as a powerful ally going forward to help shift blockages

- Recognise when frustration has gripped you in an unhelpful way

- Consider what is frustrating you now and how much of that you can turn to good effect

REGRETS

Regrets are an inevitable part of life; it is how we move on from them that matters.

The idea

Regrets are inevitable. We do not always make the right decisions or say the right things. Each week we regret some things we did. It is what we do with those regrets that matters. All religious traditions have an element of confession. As we confess what we have done wrong we are enabling ourselves to move on from those mistakes. Hence the importance of naming regrets and seeking to put them in the past rather than being dominated by them in the present.

We can be at risk of being overwhelmed by our regrets. We may develop a myth that one inappropriate comment in a meeting has damaged our whole career. We can so easily end up blowing a particular regret completely out of proportion and blaming ourselves for ruining our career or reputation in one ill-judged moment.

It is rarely the case that one comment has devastated a career, but our human psyche quite likes to find a simple explanation for our worries. It is worth being alert to how gripped we are by our regrets and the extent to which we can handle regrets in a constructive way.

A good leader will be able to say openly that they regretted certain decisions but learnt a lot from the consequences. What caused the regret will have influenced you and caused you pain. The question is, how much you have moved on from that pain, or is there a continuing niggle that needs to be addressed?

Aisha sometimes regretted that she had not done a master's degree. She regretted not being adventurous enough in both her personal and professional life. When she was tired the regrets filled too much of her thinking space. When the regrets were in the ascendency Aisha knew she needed to go for a run. After brisk exercise she could put her regrets into perspective. Yes, it might have been good to do a master's degree; yes, she could have been more adventurous, but she now had an interesting role where she could make authoritative contributions. She told herself she needed to move on from these regrets and be thankful for the opportunities she now had.

In practice

- What are the regrets you are most conscious of?

- How do you keep regrets in proportion?

- When in the past have you been conscious of a regret and then moved on from that regret in a constructive way?

- How best do you enable others to leave their regrets behind?

- How might you apply to yourself the advice you give to others on handling regrets?

FEAR OF SUCCESS AND ITS CONSEQUENCES

IT IS WELL WORTH understanding why you might be ambivalent about success.

The idea

One day we aspire to being successful; the next day success does not look attractive. We long for promotion, but may be hesitant about the resulting responsibilities.

We may have a genuine apprehension that it will take time to build up the competence and confidence to do a more senior job well, but there might also be an emotional fear that holds us back. Stepping into the unknown is an exciting adventure for some and a daunting prospect for others. Success brings opportunity, influence and authority. It also brings accountability, weighty responsibility and liabilities. When you walk up to the top of a cliff overlooking the sea you have a great view, but you recognise there is a long way to fall.

One risk is being so enmeshed in ambition that you do not appreciate some of the negative consequences of success. The opposite risk is to be so apprehensive about the consequences of success that you are wary of being adventurous. Getting the right balance is about being clear why you want to seek success and what are the qualities you bring, alongside an honest assessment of both the factual and emotional consequences for you.

What matters is being able to balance the fulfilment and joy that will flow from success for you, alongside living with the pressures, responsibilities and limitations that success will bring. It involves bringing a combination of optimism and realism, alongside adventure and groundedness.

Aisha aspired to lead a team of accountants in the firm. She thought she had the intellectual and personal qualities to be able to do that well, but was apprehensive about the expectations that would then be placed on her. Would she be able to cope with the myriad of demands? Would she be able to be fully committed as both an accountant and a senior manager? She observed others in such roles and recognised the pressures upon them.

Aisha was a touch fearful of success, but worked through how she would handle a team leader role and was clear about the type of leadership she would bring. She developed a clear narrative about her role as a team leader and her different contributions and how she would handle the accountabilities. She applied for the next team leader role confident in her ability to do the job well.

In practice

- Recognise why you want to be successful and what attributes and experience will help deliver that success

- Identify the consequences of success for you in terms of the responsibilities and expectations upon you

- Reflect on the extent to which those responsibilities inspire you or lead to inner fears

- Seek to distinguish between nervousness on the one hand and fear on the other

- Talk through with others whether these fears might be unfounded

SECTION D
GENERATE FORWARD MOMENTUM

FOCUS ON PERSONAL OBJECTIVES

ADDRESSING YOUR WORK OBJECTIVES is important, but focusing on your personal objectives is equally important.

The idea

In any good organisation you will have work objectives. If they are unclear it is worth clarifying these objectives so that expectations about what you are to deliver are agreed. There may be times when work objectives are unspecific because of external uncertainties. It is helpful if the expectations on you are as clear as possible so your progress and performance are assessed in relation to agreed expectations.

Any good appraisal system will include scope for personal development objectives as well as work objectives. It is worth tying in the organisation, of which you are a part, into a clear understanding of the next steps in your personal development. A valuable starting point is to define personal development objectives that are specifically related to your current role. This will give legitimacy to any financial cost or time commitment. This might include relevant training or coaching, work-shadowing someone in a similar role, contributing to a different part of the organisation, developing a corporate contribution, or making presentations to wider groups.

A good organisation will be interested in your long-term development as well as your short-term development, hence the importance of your thinking through what type of development will equip you for the type of activities you aspire to undertake in the longer term.

John was the development director for a health charity who was respected for his contributions and commitment. He kept himself up to date attending workshops and reading recent books and journals on the development of charitable work. His ultimate goal was to become the chief executive of a health charity and he recognised that he needed to develop his independence as a leader and better understand how chief executives could be at their most effective. He got agreement from his boss that he could go to a three-day workshop for prospective chief executives run by a business school. He put in place plans to work-shadow a couple of charity chief executives and began to think through what type of chief executive he would be.

In practice

- Is there more scope to agree with your boss personal development objectives?

- What type of personal development would equip you in the short term to do your job well?

- What type of personal development would best fit with your aspirations for the longer term?

- How do you ensure you set aside enough time for your long-term personal development?

32

DEMONSTRATE PROGRESS

When you can demonstrate progress to yourself and others you can begin to generate forward momentum.

The idea

Vague aspirations of anticipated progress soon fail to convince. What matters is measurable progress. For your own self-esteem you need to identify the progress you are making. If you are learning a foreign language you need the reassurance that you are beginning to learn vocabulary and tenses. If you feel you are making no progress the will to keep going can evaporate surprisingly quickly. Breaking progress down into small steps has the risk of making a task look more demanding than it is, but there is a benefit for most of us in marking progress on a regular basis.

A sports team will celebrate its success after each goal and not wait for the completion of the match. There is measurable progress each time it scores a goal. A team that has identified a sequence of measurable interim goals is more likely to keep up its commitment and energy.

If you are to build a reputation for delivering outcomes it is helpful to have a sequence of observable interim measures of progress to help maintain the confidence of those sponsoring the work you are doing. Once an interim outcome has been reached it is in your interest and that of your team for that progress to be recognised. The recognition is important for the morale of the team and for your long-term reputation. Ideally you want the progress that you and your team have made to be clear in reports and reviews that others make, rather than you having to describe your own accomplishments.

John built a regular reporting system so that the results from the development work were obvious to the chief executive and the trustees. This meant that figures for successful months were just as obvious as figures for less successful months. John thought this visibility of progress was right both for the organisation and for his team. This transparency meant that he did not have to assert progress in his area as the results were plain for all to see.

In practice

- Seek to ensure that progress measures are in place for your area of work

- Create an expectation that progress will be reviewed on a regular basis

- Be transparent about progress, acknowledging the contribution of others and recognising what further action is needed

- Chunk up progress into small measurable steps if possible

- Use moments when progress is reviewed to reinforce approaches that will best ensure successful outcomes

ANTICIPATE TWISTS AND TURNS

33

THE MORE WE CAN ANTICIPATE twists and turns the greater the likelihood that we will keep up consistent momentum.

The idea

The road cyclist will have ridden a route to understand its twists and turns before competing in an important road race. The cyclist will have planned when they need to take a bend slowly and how to handle the sequence of twists as the road descends sharply into a valley. The cyclist recognises that any interesting route will include twists and turns – they are part of the challenge of competing in a road race. The twists are not an unnecessary waste of time. The road cyclist has deliberately chosen road racing with its twists and turns, rather than track racing, where the bends are entirely predictable.

Part of the satisfaction of an interesting job is addressing the twists and turns with confidence. Twists and turns need to be seen as a necessary part of a job, allowing you to show your paces and handle corners with care and precision.

Handling twists and turns is for the stout-hearted, not for the faint-hearted. We will not be able to anticipate every twist or turn but often we can anticipate what might happen and prepare for it.

A role with no twists and turns can become boring and debilitating. Having to take sharp corners or handle a sequence of twists because of changing priorities gives us an inner satisfaction that we can handle any twist or turn that is next on our journey.

John recognised that there would always be ups and downs in the level of income received by the charity. He could predict some of the likely ups and downs during the financial year, with an increase before Christmas and a drop in the summer. He recognised that levels of giving are subject to wider events and which particular charitable causes are currently catching the public's imagination.

John could anticipate the reaction of his chief executive and the trustees in months when donations were lower. He would help them adjust their expectations in the light of what was likely to happen. He worked hard with foundations to build up an understanding of how best to seek their support and whether they were likely to cease their support.

In practice

- See handling twists and turns as a worthwhile part of your journey

- Think through how best to anticipate twists and turns in advance

- Prepare people both mentally and emotionally for twists and turns that might happen

- Remember that the more you can anticipate twists and turns and use your understanding to inform your contribution, the stronger your reputation will become.

34 KEEP YOUR FOCUS

Success in the moment depends on maintaining your focus and avoiding unnecessary distraction.

The idea

When I moved into coaching I taught myself to be entirely focused on the person I was working with at that moment. Being fully present in a coaching conversation requires giving someone undivided attention, so you can absorb what you hear and the emotions that are being transmitted.

The ability to focus on the task at hand and not be distracted is a key quality in building success. Bringing a focused resolve to solve a problem and a clear determination to reach the next stage builds confidence in yourself and the confidence of others in you. It is important to develop the ability to discriminate between irrelevant distraction and new information that is important for success. The ability to park a distraction for later and to think through a new piece of information in a dispassionate way is part of developing our ability to focus effectively.

The ability to multi-task is perhaps a myth that some people like to perpetuate. It is more helpful to think about the capacity to focus in a constructive way on one task and then be able to switch to another task in a timely and clear-headed way and then to a third task without losing your cool or your overall momentum. What matters is being deliberate in when you choose to switch focus and purposeful in ensuring the focus is only diluted when you choose to do so.

John recognised that the charity trustees were interested in a range of different development possibilities. If he thought about them all at the same time he would make no worthwhile progress. He had to chunk up both his time and brain space so he focused on different development opportunities in turn, having prioritised them in his own mind. He knew that he was prone to distraction, with his curiosity being both a strength and a liability.

John structured his diary so that he kept his focus on the priority areas, dealing with them sequentially. He was content saying to a trustee that he was going to focus on a particular day on a specific development opportunity. His confidence and reputation were strong enough to enable him to be firm in the way he allocated his time.

In practice

- What are the distractions you have to be most alert to?

- How best do you chunk up your time so you focus on key priorities sequentially?

- What environment enables you to focus most effectively?

- How might you reward yourself for focusing effectively on one priority at a time?

CREATE ALLIANCES AND PARTNERSHIPS

THE MORE YOU CREATE alliances the wider you can spread your influence. The more you create partnerships the greater your momentum.

The idea

Who might have a similar interest as you about the outcomes you want to deliver? You might be teaching in a school with another person teaching a parallel class: what is the best type of alliance so you are not duplicating each other's work? Perhaps one person might prepare material on maths and the other person material on English? Perhaps you and a colleague are both leading similar projects: how much can you share certain resources and seek specialist input that works effectively for both of you?

Where can we build an alliance, and how can we maximise our contribution? If as a middle manager there are a number of people who think that some changes are needed in the way the organisation is run, you can perhaps build common cause. Perhaps two or three of you can represent the interests of the whole group, or a number of you might express similar concerns to a range of different people, thereby helping to build a case that change needs to happen.

Creating a partnership with individuals or an organisation that brings a complementary level of expertise can help enhance the prospects of your reaching outcomes you want to see happen. We might think that building a wider partnership will dilute our contribution, but the reality is that it is likely to widen the impact of our contribution instead. Often we think we can achieve a lot alone, when the pragmatic reality is that we need to build alliances and partnerships if we are to have any prospect of success.

John recognised that his health charity would have limited impact on its own. It needed to be operating jointly with other charities and with the Government Department for Health if its contribution was to have its fullest effect. John took a lot of pride in the work of his charity and wanted success for both the charity and his part within it, but what mattered most was addressing the health issues that the charity was set up to engage with.

Always coming back to the deeper purpose of the charity helped John keep a focus on what type of alliances and partnerships would enable the charity to have its biggest impact. Sometimes he felt some of his trustees were more concerned about the reputation of the charity than addressing the health issue which was the purpose of the charity.

In practice

- See establishing a partnership as an opportunity and not a threat

- Seek to build alliances where each individual or group brings a distinctive and valued contribution

- Recognise when a partnership is beginning to lose its momentum and be willing to rejuvenate it or withdraw

36 USE A COACH WELL

PURPOSEFUL CONVERSATIONS with a coach can be a time-effective way of clarifying next steps.

The idea

A good coach can help an individual or team develop clarity about their next steps. Using a coach effectively depends on good preparation, purposeful conversations, crystallising attitudes and inhibitions, and clarifying what actions will make the biggest difference. A good coaching conversation is robust, engaging and purposeful.

Using a coach well will include one-to-one conversations, focused e-mail and text exchanges on specific issues, the coach observing you in action in order to be able to give specific feedback and the coach seeking views about your impact from those around you.

Good-quality coaching conversations will be about your being at your best, stepping up effectively, leaving behind dated notions about yourself, capturing and addressing the apprehensions that hold you back and enabling your motivation and energy to be directed at key priorities and not just the urgent and immediate.

Coaching conversations that work well enable you to keep up your forward momentum and have clarity about what you are learning. They can help in developing the leadership narrative that is going to be authentic for you going forward, and the stretching aspirations that will enable you to contribute in ways you judge most important. Good coaching conversations will help take your approach to a much more influential level.

John used an experienced coach as a sounding-board. John respected the coach's knowledge of both the charity and health worlds. The coach never told John what to do but shared insights and observations. The coach's questions and engagement allowed John to develop his attitude and approach to forthcoming issues.

The coaching conversations also allowed John to think about what he would do if he was a chief executive. This enabled him to balance the strategic and the day-to-day more effectively. The clearer he was about what he would do if he was a chief executive, the more confident he became in asserting these views from his role as development director.

In practice

- See coaching conversations as an important investment and not an indulgence

- Prepare effectively for coaching conversations and crystallise your conclusions at the end of the sessions

- Expect demanding questions and a searching conversation when you meet with your coach

- Be focused in the way you use coaching conversations to explore the link between deep-seated attitudes and future actions

- Be open to your attitudes and actions being radically altered as a result of coaching conversations

37 ENSURE PERSONAL SUPPORT

THE QUALITY OF YOUR personal support is central to keeping up forward momentum.

The idea

You pride yourself on being self-reliant. You have delivered a sequence of difficult tasks well and do not want to be over-dependent on other people. On the other hand you observe effective leaders being well supported by others. They may have a chief-of-staff looking after day-to-day matters, or an executive assistant managing their diary and e-mails, or an analyst providing them with up-to-date information. Good support arrangements are adaptable, responsive and practical.

The good leader will be conscious about what it is only they can do and how best they can ensure effective support from others to deliver a myriad of tasks effectively.

Personal support starts with practical support, but also includes intellectual and emotional support. Who is the person I can talk a difficult issue through with who will help me be aware of the pitfalls and put me in the direction of relevant experts? Who might I talk to whose energy and enthusiasm will be infectious, so that I can engage positively in dealing with a difficult issue? Who can I talk to whose calmness and measured approach will help settle me and enable me to develop the resolve to see an issue through to conclusion?

Ensuring you have the right type of personal support is a necessary part of being equipped to handle the expectations upon you and to have the mental space to explore longer-term issues.

John recognised that the charity wanted to keep its administrative expenditure to a minimum but he was wasting a lot of time on diary management. He persuaded his colleagues that they needed a better, electronic diary management system with someone dedicated to working as an executive assistant for three directors to ensure that their time was used effectively and that the right papers were available for key meetings.

John built a mutual mentoring relationship with a development director in another health charity, which provided valuable peer support and challenge. He identified who to talk to within the charity when he needed encouragement. He knew that five minutes with a couple of people could lift his spirits and renew his energy for the rest of the day.

In practice

- See personal support as a crucial investment and be deliberate about how you use it

- Keep adapting your personal support arrangements to fit new circumstances and do not let them fossilise

- Do not be shy about asking others to support you, but always explain why you are doing it and acknowledge why you appreciate their help

- Beware if you see personal support as selfish indulgence rather than sensible investment

CONTINUE TRAINING

SUCCESSFUL ATHLETES NEVER stop training, so as to continually improve their performance in the short and long term.

The idea

The successful athlete will have a training routine that works well for them. The training is always geared to keeping a reasonable level of fitness and resilience, but will vary depending on how close they are to a major tournament. Even in the off season the training will continue, although it might be about building up core strength rather than speed. When the athlete trains they are looking to succeed in the longer term as they build up their strength, physique and endurance.

Building success in our lives involves training for the longer term. It means strengthening your core capabilities and building an adaptability to be able to respond appropriately in a range of different circumstances. Just as the golfer keeps practising their swing, so the good committee chair continues to practise the art of chairing and refining the techniques they use.

The athlete is often building up their capacity for physical and mental endurance. For those who want to move into demanding leadership roles, building up endurance is an important prerequisite. Endurance grows through being part of teams going through tough situations and carefully calibrating your learning.

Successful cycling teams talk of continuous refinements ultimately leading to outstanding results. The cycling team will train in different combinations and have trust in each other as they continually change places in the peloton. The training for the cyclist is both about them as individuals and about the team operating together effectively.

John was a triathlete. Cycling and running came naturally to him but he had to keep up the swimming training. In the swimming leg of the triathlon most people were passing him. This experience put his ego firmly in its place and reminded him that there were some skills which, however hard you try, you can only be average at. In contrast his cycling became ever stronger with training leading to steady improvement.

John recognised that in his work there were some skills in which he would never be brilliant, which included his use of IT. There were other areas where continuous experience meant he became ever more influential, such as in giving speeches. In both of these types of areas he recognised that he needed to keep learning and practising new skills.

In practice

- What type of training works for you in sporting endeavours?

- What type of training helps you be effective in your work?

- What sort of training do you observe other people doing from which you can learn?

- Where do you need to keep practising your effectiveness?

39 PACE YOUR MOMENTUM CAREFULLY

W E   C A N   B E   I N   D A N G E R   O F either wanting to rush forward, or standing back too much.

The idea

We can view our momentum like a tank of fuel which is to be used responsibly. If we accelerate up a steep hill we use a higher proportion of fuel but can then pace more steadily down the subsequent slope. Sometimes pushing down the accelerator is necessary to get the momentum going and keep up reasonable progress on a tough climb. Sometimes increasing the momentum is about demonstrating that progress is possible and that a team can work together well.

Sometimes it is right to slow down the momentum in order to assess external data and review different opportunities. It might be time to take stock and think about problems in a different way. We need to have reflective conversations both inside a team and with other people, and then we need to regroup. We need time to let the brain reflect and see whether it comes up with a different combination of possibilities that might work well for us in the future.

It can be helpful if the leader deliberately sets the pace, just as a conductor controls the pace of an orchestra. Your success can depend on recognising the pace at which the leader wants to take forward the next movement and responding sensitively to that lead.

There is always a risk that we see fast momentum as good and slow momentum as bad. But going downhill too fast is dangerous, just as pushing a successful product too strongly can be counter-productive.

We need to judge the momentum that we need to set in order to bring people with us. If we lose their support and end up operating alone, our momentum can soon be dissipated. In any given week there will be different activities that we need to pace selectively, so that we do not exhaust ourselves by 3 p.m. A similar cycle might apply over a month or a year. Sometimes a slower momentum in the summer or in January can enable us to reflect on progress and build a plan for the future.

John knew that he needed to pace his development campaigns or he would end up with donor exhaustion. He needed to target particular groups at particular times. He needed to be innovative in the way he presented the case for the charity so that people would want to read the stories he was telling. He understood that he needed to push hard at key moments and catch people's imagination. But he recognised that if you had no fresh, interesting stories to share it was better to keep quiet and not be boringly repetitive.

In practice

- Be mindful whether your natural preference is to go too fast or too slow

- Observe how others pace their momentum and see how you can learn from them

- Accept that sometimes it is right to be going slower, in order eventually to be able to go faster

- Be mindful of what sort of pacing works best for your followers so that they want to follow you but are not exhausted in the process

KEEP SOMETHING IN RESERVE

IF YOU ARE ALWAYS operating at full throttle there is no capacity left to deal with the unexpected.

The idea

It is hard to keep a reserve of energy. We want to have an impact and get things done. We want to persuade others of the success of our cause. We want to think ahead and plan effectively for the next major event. We want to bring people with us and convert as many people as possible to our way of thinking.

We can believe in our rhetoric so much and be so passionate about our cause that we become exhausted. We learn to handle our exhaustion, just, and then operate at the boundaries of our wellbeing, teetering between full throttle and tiredness. We are flat out going forward one moment and flat out on our backs the next.

Success in the long term demands a different approach. We do need to be fully committed to whatever we are doing, but we also need to be building up our store of energy and our ability to be responsive and creative when the unexpected happens. Ideally we are operating at 85% capacity and not 120% capacity. This might mean being more selective in what we do and saying no more often.

I am often struck how senior leaders who have had to work within constrained hours for a period because of family illness quickly adapt their approach and priorities to the constrained hours. They rapidly force themselves to be more selective and use the momentum in a more focused way. When personal circumstances improve and they go back to working regular hours the challenge is whether they revert to type, or whether they continue to be selective in the way they apply their momentum. The test is whether they can then keep this available capacity in reserve for the future, or dissipate it in the way they did in the past.

The most successful leaders are always able to keep something in reserve for moments when they need to be at their best. This is a salutary lesson when we are inclined to be permanently hyperactive.

John had to pace himself after he broke his leg as he could not rush around. He needed to be selective in the meetings he attended and how he used his time. He was much more disciplined about his priorities and pleasantly surprised by what he was still able to deliver. When he returned to working full-time he put constraints into his diary and built a different understanding about his availability. The result was that following a national health scare he was able to put in a significant amount of time and energy into a new information campaign. He had built up energy reserves which he was now able to deploy wisely.

In practice

- What is the risk that you naturally operate at the extremes of your physical and mental capacity?

- What have you learnt about the way you prioritise when you have been constrained by circumstances that limited the amount of time you were able to give to work?

- How much energy and mental thinking space are you able to keep in reserve for the unexpected?

- When the unexpected happens, how will you use your physical, mental and emotional reserves effectively?

SECTION E
HANDLE SETBACKS WITH CARE

SEE MOMENTS OF FAILURE AS INEVITABLE

WE LEARN THROUGH a combination of succeeding and failing. If we are not having moments of failure we are probably not experimenting enough.

The idea

We think the ideal is to embark on a predictable pathway to ultimate success. We might be apprehensive about moments of failure and think that such incidents will throw us off course, but failure is not only inevitable it is also desirable. We learn far more through our setbacks than our successes. It is when we learn hard lessons that we adjust our attitudes and approach. Our resolve grows when we encounter setbacks.

An athlete will win some races and lose others. Through following the example of athletes who run faster they fine-tune their approach. Handling defeat is part of the life of an athlete. Those who are ultimately successful know how to cope with defeat and move graciously forward, turning defeat into a measured training programme.

A scientist will go through hundreds of 'failed' experiments before they create the chemical combination that becomes the medication prescribed by doctors. The experiment that fails is proof that a particular combination of chemicals is not where success lies.

The belief that failure is inevitable is not a justification to go into project meetings or presentations unprepared. Effective preparation sits alongside an acceptance that your contribution will never be perfect, as there is always room for improvement.

Alison was an experienced IT project leader. She had led one particular health project that had been aborted, which cost the taxpayer thousands of pounds. Various factors had contributed to this failure, including unrealistic expectations about the timescale and a limited supply of the right type of skills available at key moments. Alison learnt a huge amount through leading this project about specifying requirements clearly, working through risks in more detail, and being clear about how to address warning signs about progress being off course. She became much tougher and more direct as a consequence of her experience of the aborted programme.

In practice

- Assume you will experience both success and failure, and recognise that you will learn from both experiences

- Talk to others about how they have handled failure and learnt from it

- Recognise how you can reduce the risks of failure through clear expectations, effective risk management and good early warning systems

- Whenever you are part of something that fails ensure that there is a clear process of review and learning

ACCEPT SETBACKS AND PREPARE FOR THEM

WHEN YOU PLAN AHEAD allow time and emotional energy for handling setbacks.

The idea

Most projects require input from a range of different people. However sophisticated the planning and the timescale it is almost inevitable that there will be setbacks. The more 'just in time' the approach, the greater the risks of being thrown off course at key moments.

Handling setbacks is both about emotional preparedness and practical planning. Emotional preparedness is about keeping calm while retaining your resolve. It can mean not being overly invested emotionally in keeping strictly to one tight, self-imposed timetable. Emotional resilience is a quality we can develop through recognising the rhythms in ourselves and being able to anticipate when we are likely to become over-anxious and dissipate precious emotional energy in the process.

Preparing for setbacks involves a willingness to be open to Plan B or Plan C, and knowing when to hold your nerve and wait for the progress needed to be able to move to the next step.

If you can enable people to prepare for setbacks and lead sensitively when setbacks happen, you will develop followers who have confidence in you and will want to stay committed to what you are seeking to achieve. When people have confidence in your judgement about persisting with Plan A or moving to Plan B, they are likely to stick with you.

Alison viewed it as inevitable that any IT project she led would not go perfectly smoothly. There would always be setbacks. She recognised that it was all too easy to get into the blame game when there was a setback. What mattered was bringing realism about the problems and exploring different solutions through engaging participants with the right expertise as part of the conversations.

Alison recognised that people were observing her carefully when there was a setback. Their confidence levels would mirror her confidence levels. She recognised that she carried the whole team's expectation that under her leadership a way forward would be found. She found this expectation both a burden and an opportunity. She knew she would have the full commitment of her team when she was clear about next steps.

In practice

- Always seek to build in contingency time to deal with setbacks

- Recognise that how you deal with setbacks will be mirrored by people working for you

- Develop your emotional resilience muscles through your learning from each project

- Keep a record of how you handled setbacks and found a way forward

- Be willing to mentor younger, less experienced people about how best to handle and move on from setbacks

PUT SETBACKS INTO CONTEXT

It is important to be clear about the significance of a setback and its causes.

The idea

We may sometimes feel overwhelmed by a setback. For example, it could be clear that a project is going to be completed three weeks late, or a new element of expenditure committed by the chief executive is going to mean a cost overrun of £20,000. But minor setbacks need to be kept in proportion. A slightly longer timescale or a slightly higher cost should not negate the fact that a major achievement has been made.

When a project is held up there will inevitably be a risk of a blame game. Sometimes it is not worth interrogating the evidence in great detail to find where the fault lies. What matters is seeking to solve the problem and move purposefully on to the next stage. On other occasions it is crucial to get to the root of the issue as it might be endemic and blight the whole project. Sometimes calculations have to be done again from first principles and assumptions not taken for granted. There is a high likelihood that the owners of some data will be defensive and reluctant to reassess their calculations.

The good leader will bring a sharp eye about where calculations might be built on false premises. They will be willing to retest assumptions and apply a sanity check, drawing on the experience of people who have not been immersed in the issue before.

When the cause of the setback is clear to you, you may have to make yourself unpopular by being directive in exposing the problem and requiring remedial action. Being blunt and clear about expectations is part of your responsibility. Having taken this direct approach once, it will feel easier on subsequent occasions.

Alison initially thought that a contractor was to blame for a particular setback but when she began exploring the details she became uneasy about some of the underlying calculations done by members of her team. She went through the figures directly with these team members, who initially defended their calculations without hesitation.

Alison had spotted an inconsistency and eventually her team members accepted that they had made a significant error and thereby created a set of expectations that were much more difficult to deliver than they had expected. Alison worked through the procedures with these two members of staff to ensure that a similar problem did not happen again. She did not blame them, but was direct with them about her future expectations.

In practice

- Be willing to be forensic in looking for causes of setbacks

- Treat the views of participants with respect, but be bold in interrogating their evidence

- Be relentless if you think there is a problem that could be systemic and recur

- Be focused and direct without using the language of blame

44 DON'T RUSH TO CRITICAL JUDGEMENTS

INITIAL JUDGEMENTS CAN BLUR our vision and prejudice the way we assess the evidence.

The idea

The thoughtful judge tells a jury to keep an open mind and weigh up all the evidence carefully. The judge will ask jurors to leave behind views or prejudices about particular types of people and situations. They must view the evidence on its merits and then reach a conclusion.

When there is a setback in a project we are likely to have an initial view about whose fault it is. This can be a useful intuitive insight, but often it is our prejudice bursting to the surface.

Our reaction might be to see the whole project as a failure and be critical of others and ourselves. As an instant reaction, we want to point a finger at someone, but this raises hackles, creates defensiveness, and undermines trust.

The key to not rushing to critical judgements is to depersonalise an issue and look at the evidence and the potential causes and effects. The more a review can be depersonalised, the greater the likelihood that all those involved will be willing to make a useful contribution to sorting out a constructive way forward. A critical eye ought to lead to clear conclusions and thoughtful next steps. It could mean the departure of individuals from a project, but always with clear reasons.

Being publicly critical of people rarely leads to a fruitful outcome. Being forensic about how different factors were assessed and drawing clear lessons for the future is much more likely to lead to outcomes that all those with an interest can accept.

Alison handled difficult contractors skilfully. She recognised when they were seeking to put undue pressure on her. What others might have described as bullying tactics she saw as an over-aggressive presentation of their case. When they pushed their argument too hard Alison did not take this personally. She never attacked the integrity of the individual contractors. She smiled to herself about their relative naivety and always focused on the issue rather than the individual. When they tried to push her into a corner she gave them a steely look and focused the discussion on what they were going to do next rather than what she was going to do next.

In practice

- Hold back from criticising people personally

- Focus on the issue, the evidence and next steps

- If you feel under personal attack address the issue and not the other person and openly examine the scope to find a constructive solution

- When you feel under personal attack resist responding in kind

RECOGNISE YOUR EMOTIONAL REACTION TO SETBACKS

SETBACKS IN INDIVIDUAL PROJECTS can derail us, or they can enable us to think laterally about how problems can be solved.

The idea

A setback can easily affect our confidence if we are not careful. We can go into 'try harder' mode and work 14 hours a day to try to address the problem. Sometimes working long hours will be necessary, though even then it can only be sustained for limited periods. But the more we put our head down to try to solve the problem, the less likely we are to spot some of the underlying causes.

Your reaction might be to want to run away and disappear. Allowing yourself some time applying avoidance might be necessary so that you can get your equilibrium back and address issues in a logical way.

An emotional reaction that leads you to want to indulge to excess is likely to be dangerous and ultimately unrewarding. Always watch out for early warning signals about this danger.

When your emotional reaction leads you to want to talk an issue through with trusted others reflecting on what matters most to you, then you are likely to address it dispassionately, with a greater likelihood of arriving at constructive next steps.

An emotional reaction to a setback often needs to be allowed to happen. If we bottle up emotions too much they are likely to burst out in unhelpful ways. Our emotional reactions can give us resolve and energy to bring solutions rather than being overwhelmed by the problems. Learning how to handle our emotional reaction to setbacks and use them constructively is at the heart of building success over a sustained period. We need passion and enterprise to create successful outcomes. But being enlivened by our emotions and not undermined by them is not always straightforward. Our emotional response can inspire us one minute and undermine us the next.

Alison was conscious she had strong emotions just below the surface. There was a strong emotional commitment to deliver whatever the setback. But on occasion there could be an overwhelming emotion of gloom and despondency. Alison was aware of her pattern of emotional reactions and could normally anticipate when a strong emotion would kick in.

Alison was conscious when she needed to take a short, brisk walk to contain emotions of frustration or anger. She had trained herself to be measured in her responses. She recognised that her emotions brought passionate commitment to what she was doing, which was crucial for her success. She was willing to accept that holding her emotions at bay was not straightforward.

In practice

- Accept that your emotional reactions to setbacks are a key part of who you are

- See the value and strength of your positive emotional reactions and the value of an emotional reaction that means you believe major change is needed

- Know your rhythms and be conscious of your likely emotional reactions before they happen

RECOGNISE THE PERSONAL DAMAGE FROM SETBACKS

SOMETIMES SETBACKS DAMAGE your personal reputation in a way that is difficult to redeem.

The idea

Sometimes events happen outside your control and you are held responsible. You are ultimately accountable for the work of your team. If things go wrong under your watch you are rightly held to account.

I had a successful record as a Finance Director for a Government Department over a four-year period. Just before I moved to another role an error was made in some financial calculations, which meant we committed, as a Department, more funds than we had available at that time. Although I was then in a new role I was conscious this error had happened under my watch; I took responsibility to tell the Secretary of State of the error. I knew that this unfortunate incident would inevitably affect my personal reputation but it was absolutely right to take full responsibility and ensure that lessons were learnt in order to minimise the risk of such an occurrence happening again.

If something goes wrong on your watch you rightly have to accept personal accountability as you are ultimately responsible for the procedures and standards that were adopted. There may be damage to your reputation in the short term – that is a fact of life – but if you seek to hide the mistake or blame someone else the damage to your reputation is likely to be greater. You have to live with the reality that it takes a long time to build up a positive reputation and quite a short time for it to be dented.

Alison had suffered reputational damage because of the aborting of the health IT project that she was leading. This would always be on her record. She addressed this inevitability by making clear what she had learnt from the experience, sharing that experience with others and seeking to ensure she minimised the prospect of similar problems occurring in future projects. Alison lived with the view that demonstrating conspicuous, on-going competence was what mattered, and this particular health project eventually receded into history.

In practice

- Be emotionally prepared for the inevitability that something will go wrong on your watch, with you having to accept responsibility for that setback

- When you are going through a period where things are running smoothly keep building up your credit and your reputation

- When something goes badly wrong be visibly accountable and ensure a thorough review about what happened so lessons can be learnt

KNOW HOW YOU WILL HANDLE RISKS IN THE FUTURE

RISK MANAGEMENT CAN EITHER be ignored or become too much of a preoccupation. Measuring and managing risks is important for long-term success.

The idea

Risk management has become an industry that generates lots of paper. Analysing risks in a bureaucratic way can absorb a huge amount of time and miss the inevitability of new, unexpected risks.

Risk assessment needs to be done systematically, and always with an eye to what new and previously unexpected risks might occur. Managing risks well involves reviewing what has happened in similar situations, identifying key uncertainties, and recognising when urgent expectations might distort priorities and increase the prospect of new risks.

It is always worth investing time in ensuring that your sponsors understand the key risks and have confidence in the measures you are taking to address those risks. Equally important is clarity in your thinking about how you will take action if some of those risks materialise. Going through a variety of contingency arrangements is always worthwhile provided it does not absorb a disproportionate amount of time. It is worth being deliberate in thinking ahead about how you handle situations that might go wrong so that your action is focused and not purely responsive.

Alison put a lot of personal attention into managing risks. She was relentless in getting members of her team to set out the detailed risks that they needed to address. Her tone was always positive in encouraging them to develop strategies to address these risks. When she felt they were not being rigorous enough she was ready to push them to be clear what their contingent arrangements would be.

In order that people were not preoccupied with risks Alison would deliberately say, after exploring a risk with someone, that the next steps were fine, and that they should be fully committed to the next phase of work and not be preoccupied with the risk. Alison would then say that in six weeks' time she would address the risk with them afresh in the light of the latest developments.

Alison was philosophical about the risks facing her. If another major project went wrong some people would link that perception with the earlier project for which she was accountable. She recognised that she had to live with this reality, shrugged her shoulders and got on with the job in hand.

In practice

- Be systematic in ensuring risks are explored

- See risk management as a crucial part of any manager's job

- Give people the confidence that most risks can be managed effectively without there being a guarantee of success

- Seek to ensure that risks are examined regularly and thoroughly, but not in a way that stops forward progress on projects

BE WILLING TO REINVENT YOURSELF

THERE ARE MOMENTS WHEN we need to regroup and decide on the type of leader we are going to be going forward.

The idea

A winger in a football team who is starting to lose a little bit of pace might reinvent themselves as a midfield player, where anticipation and quality of passing are more important than sheer speed. A tennis player who has enjoyed success at singles may become a doubles player, drawing on skill rather than power and speed around the court.

We might have built a reputation as an economist and reached as far up that profession as we are likely to go. We recognise that we do not have the intellectual equipment that would enable us to become an outstanding economist, but we are able to work effectively with people from different professions. We begin to rebrand ourselves as a general manager rather than an economist. We will always bring economist skills but in a way that is focused on operational effectiveness rather than the purity of economic analysis.

We may see the profession we are working in shrinking and decide that it is time to make a move into a different sphere. What matters is being clear what are the generic skills we are taking with us and how best they can be combined, presented and exercised.

Moments when you repackage your strengths and contribution provide the opportunity to think again about your overall values and aspirations. Now might be the moment to think anew what matters most to you in the light of your life experience and to be deliberate in choosing which next steps to take forward.

Alison had always described herself as an IT project leader but began to think this might be a limiting definition. The reality was that she was a generalist senior manager with a project management specialism. Her original skills were about IT development. The skills she used most now were about team building, negotiation, forward thinking and programme management. Her strongest skills were now about steering and enabling others rather than doing day-to-day work on projects.

Alison developed a new narrative about the leadership she brought – one which described accurately what she now did. She stopped hesitating when describing herself as a senior manager.

In practice

- Recognise that every few years your description of the leadership you bring needs to be updated

- Accept that redefining your approach in the light of changed circumstances is timely and provides a positive starting point for the future

- Use words to describe yourself that are accurate and do not box you in with a narrow definition

- Be comfortable with the fact that you are likely to be reinventing yourself again in a few years' time

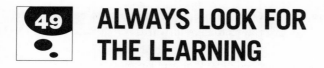

ALWAYS LOOK FOR THE LEARNING

WHATEVER THE SITUATION, however painful it is, there is always constructive learning.

The idea

When we stop wanting to learn something dies within us. We always learn more from our setbacks than we do from our successes. When I was a senior leader in Government I was good at building positive relationships and creating a sense of positive momentum but I was less effective at dealing with limited performance. In retrospect I should have been much more deliberate about handling examples of limited performance and been more open to having difficult conversations at an early stage.

A consequence is that in my second career as an executive coach I seek to enable people to work through their less strong areas and to become bolder and tougher in handling them. I can normally spot if someone is less sure-footed than they should be in handling poor performance or conflict; I seek to assist them to recognise the risks and become tougher and more assertive in these areas.

We can dwell on big setbacks that have knocked our confidence and affected our credibility. It is equally important to be aware of how we respond to daily setbacks and whether we allow them to drain us or recharge us. Every day there will be disappointments and outcomes that do not go our way. Observing the pattern can help us change the way we react. For example, we might be thrown by implied criticisms but over time develop a capacity to be amused rather than perturbed by them.

Alison kept a log of how she responded to different people and in different situations, and what she was learning as a consequence about herself. She did not do this in a morbid, introspective way. She was amused by her reactions to different situations and sought to think through whether she might handle the daily mix of demands on her in a different way so it did not feel she was going from one setback to another.

There was a risk in the past that Alison's learning was about what she should not do. Increasingly she was switching her learning into reinforcing what she did well and drawing more fully on the expertise of others.

In practice

- Seek to find the learning in any setback or disappointment, however minor

- Learn as much from the positive and how you build on your strengths, rather than dwelling on what does not go as well as you would have liked

- Keep a log of the situations you want to be able to handle more effectively going forward and then be willing to be bold in trying out new approaches

- Be willing to share your learning with others, both from successes and mistakes

BE OPEN TO CHANGING DIRECTION

THERE ARE MOMENTS WHEN it is right to change direction and not just reinvent the leadership you bring.

The idea

Sometimes when you have a setback it is right to regroup and then continue with the same aspiration. On other occasions it is right to consider a complete shift in direction.

The laboratory where you work might be closing down and there is no nearby laboratory that wants your particular scientific skills. You enjoy working with young people and apply successfully to retrain as a physics teacher.

Your career as a sportswoman is coming to an end; you train as a coach and continue in sport in a very different role.

You began teaching as a maths teacher soon after you graduated but have become bored with the classroom. An accountancy firm is seeking to recruit maths graduates and train them as accountants. You see this as an attractive change of career that will continue to use your maths expertise to good effect.

I changed direction at age 55 from being a senior government official to coaching individuals and teams. This was a radical change, moving from leading hundreds of people to having a member of a staff working for me for part of her time. I had been spending an increasing amount of time coaching emerging leaders when I was a Director General and wanted to move into coaching as a full-time job. This change of direction reinvigorated me, so that at 66 I am continuing to work full-time in my second career of executive coaching combined with being a university professor.

Changing direction may entail taking risks, losing status, being less financial secure and having less status. But if we are passionate about our new direction and can see where we can contribute, the hesitations are not likely to overwhelm us or get in the way of taking forward this change of direction in a constructive way.

Alison loved drawing the best out of the next generation. She got a buzz out of helping people develop their programme and project management skills. She considered applying for a job at a university lecturing on programme and project management, but decided that she wanted to be doing a role with a larger hands-on element than would be possible as a university lecturer.

Although Alison dismissed the idea of a switch of career into university lecturing she wanted to build into the repertoire of her activities an element of developing others. She volunteered to participate in leading training courses within the wider organisation. She set aside time to mentor younger leaders within the organisation. In the years to come she thought she might change her core focus to training and development, but not yet.

In practice

- What new direction might you consider that would use your strengths to good effect and capture your imagination?

- How might future setbacks encourage you to take forward ideas about changing direction with new resolve?

- How can you view the possibility of any future setback as potentially opening the door to a new direction?

SECTION F
BUILD YOUR REPUTATION

UNDERSTAND YOUR IMPACT

SOMETIMES THE IMPACT we have in reality is very different from our assumed impact. We need to understand how we are perceived if our contribution is to be effective.

The idea

We may see ourselves as clear and influential, but we may be perceived by others as arrogant and full of ourselves. We may think we exude charm and empathy, when people view us as fickle and unconvincing. We may believe we give people our undivided attention and listen to them intently, when we may be perceived as being too eager to move on to the next person, with no hint of apology for doing so.

We might think carefully about our impact in one situation and step unprepared into another. Paradoxically our impact might be greatest when we are at our most authentic and not preoccupied with the image we present.

We are always viewed through the lens of another person. They will bring their own presumptions and expectations. They will interpret our behaviour through the lens of their values and experiences.

We do not control the impact we have, which can be perceived as very different by different people, but we can learn to understand the impact we are likely to have on a range of people. We can assess when we are likely to inspire and when we are likely to irritate.

It is always helpful to have trusted colleagues who will give you feedback on your impact in different situations. If they can feedback how you impact on different colleagues, this can give you valuable data about when your impact is at its most effective and when you are in danger of creating negative reactions. But even they will be influenced by the lens through which they look.

It can be helpful to think through what is the view you want an influential person to have of you and then to work back to decide how you want to impact on that person. If you want a reputation as someone who gets things done, how do you evidence that capability? If you want a reputation for thinking long-term, how best do you engage in longer-term discussions so that you are seen to make valuable interventions?

Bill wanted to pursue a career in local politics and liked to express his views forcibly. He received sound advice from some experienced politicians that he needed to listen carefully to what people's concerns were before expressing strong views. Only if he pitched his arguments firmly to meet the concerns of voters would he be likely to win their support. To be convincing in his impact he needed to both understand where his hearers were coming from and be inspiring and clear in what he said.

In practice

- Recognise when your impact has been at its greatest – why did it work well?

- Appreciate how it can be counter-productive if you push your points too aggressively

- Prepare so your impact is deliberate

- Beware of over-preparing, or your approach may become stilted

- Seek feedback from trusted others about your impact

52 | APPRECIATE YOUR SUPPORTERS

YOUR REPUTATION DEPENDS ON having a range of supporters who are committed to your wellbeing and your success.

The idea

No one wins a battle alone. We all need supporters to encourage us, nurture us and challenge us. A good supporter is not sycophantic; they tell us the truth about our impact. They may be careful in choosing the right moment and selective in what they say to us, but they know when to prompt us to think afresh. A thoughtful supporter does not vote for you unquestioningly. They debate with you, express reservations and work with you on creating solutions. A good supporter will not surprise you with disloyalty but will forewarn you when the basis of their support is under strain.

The more you invest in people the more supporters you will have. If you spend time helping somebody who is facing difficulties you are likely to create an admirer for life. If you invest time in helping to develop a younger leader or someone new to a demanding role, you are likely to build respect and affection across a wide base.

It is important to keep recognising the contribution of people who are in some ways supporting you. Words of thanks for specific contributions both reinforce that quality in the individual and strengthen the relationship between you and them. Never forget that the more you explicitly acknowledge the contribution of people inside and outside your organisation the greater the likelihood that they will want to keep listening to you and support you in your future endeavours.

Always remember that the most junior people in an organisation can be the most influential in building your reputation. The doorman telling people that you always give them a bright smile can have a huge effect on your reputation across the organisation.

Bob could get grumpy when he was tired. He had a bright smile for members of the general public he met, but could be dismissive about the efforts of some of the political party workers. He wondered why some of the party workers were reluctant to talk to him. Eventually he realised it was because he was reluctant to talk to them. Because he showed little appreciation for what the party workers did, they did not rush to volunteer to help him. Bob recognised that if he was going to be successful in local politics he had to win the goodwill of volunteers so they wanted to help him. He needed to be equally committed to win the hearts and minds of party workers and potential voters.

In practice

- Remember that you always need supporters if you are going to be successful

- Be specific in the way you acknowledge the contribution of those who help you be successful

- Be careful if you appear to give a very different impression to external people you are trying to influence compared to people inside your organisation

- Allow your supporters the opportunity to influence your thinking and never be dismissive of their views

- Have regular events where you celebrate your supporters

53 CULTIVATE YOUR CHAMPIONS

WE ALL NEED CHAMPIONS in order to progress. We need influential people to speak well of our contributions and the outcomes we have helped deliver.

The idea

Each successful person will normally be able to identify a more experienced person who saw their potential, encouraged their development, mentored them through demanding times and talked openly with influential people about their potential and contribution. We all need champions in more senior roles who are willing to use their wisdom and insight to help us grow in confidence, sensitivity and courage.

A good champion will be specific in their praise and direct in their criticism. A good champion will speak the truth unequivocally, but will also focus on building an individual's resolve to focus their contribution ever more effectively.

A good champion will encourage you to step out of your comfort zone and put yourself in different situations where you are testing the boundaries of your own abilities. A good champion will review with you what has happened so your self-awareness grows and your judgement about your impact becomes more acute.

Building your champions involves investing in them. It might mean offering support when they have tasks that need to be done quickly. It might mean encouraging them when their leadership works effectively. Cultivating your champions requires investment of time and goodwill; it might also involve telling them the truth when things go wrong.

Bob thought that he was an obvious candidate to stand for election for a particular ward and was surprised when he was not everyone's first choice and was not selected. He then recognised that he needed to spend more time with senior members of the local political party helping them think through local policies. He needed to build a reputation for making constructive contributions at both policy and organisational levels.

Bob joined a number of working groups for which he was willing to write papers. He spent time listening to the chair of the local party and helped him work through a number of tricky issues. When a future by-election was announced it was the local chair of the party who suggested that Bob might be considered as a candidate. Bob recognised the value that had flowed from investing in a potential champion.

In practice

- Accept that you will always need champions to succeed

- Think carefully about who might be your champions and reflect on how you can enable these individuals to do their roles effectively

- Focus on who your champions might be, but then allow them to choose their moment to support you rather than demanding their backing

- Remember to acknowledge your previous and current champions in the years ahead, and do not forget the contribution they made to your success

54 BE CONSCIOUS OF THE GOSSIP

IT IS WORTH KNOWING what the gossip is about you. You then have a choice about how you respond to that gossip.

The idea

Everybody has a reputation within an organisation. Normally there is an element of truth in any gossip, but over time it can become elaborated, with you being depicted as a caricature of yourself. Gossip will always accentuate both the positive and the negative. From just one or two events a whole mythology about your personality and predilections can be generated.

If you are dismissive of someone who is well thought of, you may develop a reputation for treating people badly. If you are over-aggressive with a couple of people, you may develop a reputation for being arrogant or even for being a bully. If you show genuine concern for someone who is going through bereavement and spend time with them, you may be spoken of as someone who is caring and compassionate.

If you do not talk to people you are likely to be branded a recluse. If you talk too loudly in the open plan you may be gossiped about as insensitive or even odious. If you look hesitant and speak quietly in meetings the gossip might be that you lack confidence and therefore should not be given major responsibility. If you are frequently late for meetings you may be considered unreliable.

It is important to be cognisant of the signals you give, while recognising that you will be a source of gossip whether you like it or not. It is important not to be over-worried about some negative gossip as it will always be there. It is worth knowing what the gossip is about you, so you can take steps to shift the gossip in a more helpful direction, recognising that it can take quite a long time to turn negative gossip into positive comments.

Bob understood that he was seen as ambitious and sharp-elbowed. He did not mind being viewed as adventurous or ambitious. This was consistent with the signals he wanted to give, but he did not particularly like the implication that he could be arrogant. He knew he needed to build a constructive relationship with different people within the local political party. He needed to be persistently constructive and not appear dismissive of the contribution of others. He knew that people would be testing him out to see if he could be consistent in setting a constructive and encouraging tone.

In practice

- Seek to find out what is the gossip about you

- Accept that there will always be some negative gossip and accept the inevitability of this

- Remember that it takes time to build up positive gossip, but one unfortunate act is all it takes to turn gossip negative

- Recognise that if people are gossiping about you, they are taking you seriously

- Observe how the gossip about you can change over time

55 WATCH IF YOU ARE ABOUT TO LOSE YOUR COOL

THE MOST DANGEROUS, most negative reputation results from showing anger. The implication is that you can get out of control and are insensitive to your impact on others.

The idea

When you are about to lose your cool always stop and either 'bite your tongue' or take a break. Once you have shown anger in front of others you will always have a reputation for anger. As a consequence people will be much more wary about saying what they think in front of you because they do not want to suffer your ire. This inhibition can be costly if it means that issues are not addressed at an early stage in a thorough way.

An even bigger downside is the risk you are seen as somebody who is not in control of their own emotions. One of the prime limiters of progress for any leader is being seen as someone who is not able to handle larger responsibilities well and keep calm.

It is important to think through how you respond in different situations so that you are conscious when you might lose your cool. At such times you might suggest a tea break or hold off pursuing a particular topic until further information becomes available. The respite might give you the opportunity to cool down, and to have conversations with other people who also have an interest.

Sometimes you will want to express your views clearly and forcibly, but such an approach should always be deliberate and thought through, never expressed in a fit of anger.

Bob could get irritated by others in the local political party. He thought a number of them were small-minded and conceited. There were moments when he wanted to tell them to grow up and stop living in the previous century. He recognised that speaking his mind directly could be counter-productive. If he began to speak too directly he knew his voice would rise, his face would go red and people would distance themselves from him.

Bob recognised that he would have to put up with what he regarded as a small-minded approach. He recognised that if he lost his cool with loyal and committed members of the local party, he would have no future as a political candidate. Knowing this harsh reality meant that Bob retained diplomatic politeness even with the most difficult of people.

In practice

- Observe what happens to the reputation of others when they lose their cool

- Know what are the early warning signals for you that you might lose your cool

- Be ready with your personal strategies so that you calm down and do not let your anger show

- Recognise the times when you do need to be forceful, but do this in a planned and premeditated way

- Acknowledge to yourself when you have kept your cool when many others would have let their anger show

56 RECOGNISE THE IMPORTANCE OF WIN/WIN

GETTING TO THE POINT where all the parties feel they have won helps build your reputation as a negotiator and enabler of the success of others.

The idea

When someone feels defeated they may have a grudging respect for what you have done, but there might be an underlying resentment and limited trust for the future. Short-term success can lead to long-term ambivalence and distancing from others.

When there is disagreement with someone about next steps it is worth being clear what particularly matters to an individual. You may well not want to concede what you regard as the most significant point, but it can be helpful to reflect on what would help the other person feel they are not completely defeated.

An individual is likely to be sensitive about their reputation if they feel it has been damaged because they totally lost in their negotiation with you. If you are able to say you have taken account of their perspective in some tangible way, the individual has the possibility of keeping their reputation intact. It is their choice how they respond to your acknowledging points that matter to them.

Your reputation does not depend on winning every argument. Accepting the point of view of others graciously, and recognising that their preference should prevail in some situations, enhances rather than diminishes your reputation. What matters is how you win and how you respond when others win. The person who accepts defeat graciously and does not over-celebrate their success will be both respected and liked.

Bob was naturally competitive. He enjoyed team sports, especially when his side was victorious. When his football team was losing he could become aggressive, using words that he would not use in front of his children. Bob often felt in competition with other members in his political party. He liked to win arguments but saw that this approach did not always win friends. He recognised that he needed to acknowledge the points of view of others even though he wanted to put his preference clearly.

Bob learnt that to be convincing he needed to show more than grudging acceptance. He also began to recognise that although he disagreed fundamentally with some of his political opponents there was a shared interest in enabling members of the public to believe in the value of the democratic political process. He was willing to share a platform with political opponents at a further education college in order to help build interest in local politics. He saw this as an important, long-term win/win.

In practice

- Be careful if your inclination is to rub the noses of your opponents in their defeat

- See a win/win as a good outcome and not an uneasy compromise

- Keep a lookout for how you can enable others to win on points that are most important to them

- Recognise how creating win/win situations builds a long-term, positive reputation for you

57 KEEP YOUR VALUES INTACT

Whatever the aggravation or disappointment, keeping your values intact is important for your wellbeing, self-esteem and reputation.

The idea

Success is not fundamentally about status or pay. It is about how you turn your values into attitudes and actions, which produce the desired results which in turn reinforce those values. You want to build a reputation that you have kept to your values and have been able to 'hold your head up high' in a variety of demanding situations.

When you have been seen to live your values, others will notice. They might think that you could have been more pragmatic but they will respect the way you have maintained your values.

Beware lest you are seen to be inconsistent by articulating one value while having acted inconsistently with that value on a previous occasion. The person who argues the importance of honesty and integrity will have their actions scrutinised to see whether they truly live their values. If there are blemishes on their record, a dogmatic assertion of the values of integrity and honesty, without an element of the confessional, is likely to be unconvincing.

When you feel under pressure it is always worth asking yourself what your values are telling you is the right thing to do in the situation. You might take account of the timing and the emotions of others before taking what you think is the right step forward, but reflecting on the values that are most important to you in any situation gives you a framework within which to decide on your next actions.

An important value for Bob was respect for individuals. Applying this value was straightforward when it came to political speeches about the need to respect personal choices and providing social care that respected the circumstances of individuals. Respecting some members of his political party was more of a challenge. He kept feeling dismissive of the small-mindedness of some of his party colleagues, but he knew he needed to respect their views, because it was the right thing to do and because it was necessary for party harmony.

Bob initially had difficulty respecting his political opponents and was sometimes tempted to be rude to them. He recognised that he wanted to be treated with respect by his political opponents. If this was to happen he needed to show respect to his opponents. The result was that he was more willing to act jointly with some of his political opponents on some issues because of mutual intent and growing respect.

In practice

- In a difficult situation be willing to ask what are your overriding values that are relevant in the context

- Recognise the importance of being consistent in the way you apply your values

- Be open about your underlying values and encourage people to give you feedback on whether you have applied them

- See it as more important to live your values than win an argument

58 BE HONEST WHEN YOU MAKE MISTAKES

ADMITTING YOUR MISTAKES AND being clear how you have learnt from them helps enhance your reputation for humility and continual improvement.

The idea

When we make a mistake the initial human reaction is to cover it up. We feel our reputation will be tarnished if there is a litany of mistakes attached to our name. Politicians are often reluctant to admit mistakes as they believe the media will repeat those mistakes relentlessly, with their reputation suffering permanent damage as a result.

In contrast the young manager who is willing to be open about the mistakes they have made will be viewed as someone worth developing and investing in. Their reputation is enhanced when they are able to demonstrate how they have learnt from their mistakes, and are seen to be tackling similar situations in a different way.

A key part of learning from mistakes is being honest with yourself when an approach is not working. There is a risk that we keep focusing on a particular way of doing things with the belief that if we keep trying harder we will make the unlikely happen. Sometimes the mistake is about being too relentless and single-minded. Perhaps we have to view a situation afresh and apply a different approach.

Sometimes when we make mistakes others will feel we have let them down. Recognising the emotional reaction of others and speaking into that emotional reaction is important for keeping our reputation intact. When people are disappointed with us we need to accept that this is an inevitable emotional reaction and they will need time and encouragement from us to move through the emotional reaction.

Bob had always been reluctant to admit his mistakes. When he failed to make a good tackle on the football pitch he would blot out this mistake from his mind and not apologise to himself or his colleagues.

When Bob made the mistake of being over-dogmatic with some senior members of the local political party he was initially reluctant to admit it. He sensed there was a degree of animosity towards him and talked this through with the chair of the local party, admitting that he had been over-dogmatic in some situations. The party chair respected Bob's openness and honesty and gave him good advice, encouraging him to build an alliance with a couple of senior members of the local party and to admit his mistaken approach openly and not begrudgingly. Once Bob acted on this advice, a new constructive rapport developed quite quickly as these individuals had an underlying admiration for him.

In practice

- Accept that the most powerful learning comes from mistakes we make

- Observe how others describe their mistakes and their resulting learning

- Be open in the way you articulate how you have learnt from your mistakes and how you have changed your approach

- Be mindful about the disappointment of others when they observe your mistakes and then help them move from disappointment into understanding your learning

WIDEN YOUR REPUTATION

It is worth thinking deliberately about how you widen your reputation and the number of people who know about your contribution.

The idea

We feel uncomfortable about marketing ourselves and deliberately widening our reputation. The resultant risk is that others are unaware of how we can contribute. Our reputation may stay localised and our influence be much smaller than it might be.

We may be known for one particular type of contribution. Part of widening our reputation is developing a range of skills and approaches and having clear evidence of how they have been applied successfully. When I prepare people for interview I encourage them to develop a full and honest narrative about the range of contributions they have made in different situations. I encourage them to enter an interview confidently, ready to tell a range of stories giving evidence of the contributions they have made and the outcomes they have helped to deliver.

For most people the risk is their reputation is based on their last success or their last failure. It is important to have a narrative that describes more fully your contribution in a number of spheres over a number of years, and to be willing to share that experience in mentoring conversations, in groups, or speaking from a public platform.

When I work with someone who has just started a new role I encourage them to think about who are the people who will be important to their success. I encourage the newly appointed person to seek to build relationships with these interlocutors, listening carefully to them and sharing their own stories, expectations and aspirations. Building your reputation with people new to you needs to come across as genuine engagement and not as a means to an end.

While Bob was well known within his local political party, he recognised that he needed to build a reputation across a wider network. He volunteered to go to the national party conference and made contact there with a range of different politicians. He offered to take part in a national working group. He was willing to read the papers and seek a range of views before going to the meetings. He gradually built a reputation for understanding the wider perspectives within the political party and for contributing constructive points at a national level drawn from his local experience.

In practice

- Understand whether your reputation is based on others' limited understanding about what you contribute

- Think through how you want to widen your contribution in your current role so your reputation covers a wider mix of qualities

- Think through who you want to build a reputation with and seek to build a relationship with them

- Have a clear narrative about what your strengths are and the outcomes you have delivered and be ready to draw from this narrative selectively

- Be open to new and different ways in which you can contribute to causes or outcomes that are important to you

60 RENEW YOUR PROFILE

THERE IS A RISK that we project an outdated view of ourselves and do not catch up with the distinctive contribution that we are now able to bring.

The idea

We might brand ourselves as a good project manager and have some favourite stories about the impact we have had and the contribution we have made. A risk is that these stories brand us in a way that is out of date. At heart we are a project manager; what we do now is enable others to lead projects well. At heart we may think of ourselves as a classroom teacher; what we are particularly gifted at now is encouraging and motivating other teachers and thinking ahead in a constructive way so that we can plan the curriculum for other teachers to implement.

You have built up a wealth of experience and insight. Perhaps the time has come to take a lead in chairing a working group or speaking at a local event. It might be opportune to offer to write an article or write a blog.

Your CV or profile on a social networking website can become outdated surprisingly quickly. Refreshing the way we present ourselves orally and in writing is important. We can easily become and sound stale.

I am not encouraging you to be a chameleon, always adjusting to the colours and moods of the day, but I am encouraging you to look consistently at the interrelationship between the competences and insights you bring and the changing needs and circumstances of the spheres you are engaged within. If you pride yourself on being adaptable and spontaneous it helps if you are able to demonstrate your adaptability and spontaneity, and respond well to changing opportunities and expectations.

Bob was known for expressing strong local political views. Having been part of a couple of national working groups he recognised that he could bring a wider perspective. He deliberately modified the way he contributed locally so he was drawing on both his national and local experience. The consequence was that his views were taken more seriously and he became more influential, reinforcing for him the value of this approach. His reputation could now have two strands rather than one: he was a local activist and he brought national insights.

In practice

- Be mindful if your description of your strengths has not been updated for a long time

- Recognise when your description of yourself is out of date

- Celebrate how your contribution has changed and evolved in recent months

- Experiment with describing your distinctiveness in different ways with different people to see which description feels most authentic and up to date

SECTION G
BALANCE THE SHORT TERM AND THE LONG TERM

BE WILLING TO HANDLE THE IMMEDIATE

A REPUTATION FOR CAPABILITY is reliant on your being able to handle the immediate calmly and effectively.

The idea

The prevailing narrative is that a good leader is able to think strategically and bring insights relevant to the longer term. But the bedrock of success for a good leader is to be able to handle the immediate calmly and effectively. Ignoring the immediate as beneath you or boring is just as dangerous as spending all your time in the immediate.

Whatever the quality of our forward thinking, our basic reputation will depend on whether we do the day job well. Others will listen to our views on the longer term if they have confidence in our ability to keep day-to-day issues under control.

We can sometimes be thrown emotionally by expectations about the immediate that are placed upon us. We feel bombarded with questions, e-mails, and requests for five minutes of our time. We cannot ignore these pleas for help or requests for steers. It is an essential part of our role to be available and responsive to the needs of the moment.

Someone might need a quick steer on what they say to a customer. A journalist may be asking for our view on a current event. An important stakeholder has asked about a particular priority and the answer is in your head and not on a piece of paper.

There can be a varied mix of perfectly reasonable requests which, if viewed in totality, would be exhausting. Handling the immediate is about rationing your time, focusing your interventions, and being fully absorbed in an issue for five minutes and trusting your instinctive response. It includes deciding when it is time for you to act and when someone else should take forward the next action. Success comes through recognising that dealing with the immediate is part of your job and important to handle well, but is not the totality of your responsibility.

Lin was the administrative manager responsible for the operating theatres in a hospital. Her life was full of immediate requests. She recognised that she was dealing with life-and-death situations and relished dealing with the immediate. She recognised when she needed to intervene and when she should place clear expectation on someone else to sort a problem out. She had learnt over recent years how to be more selective in her use of time so that she handled the immediate without feeling controlled or overwhelmed by it.

In practice

- See dealing with the immediate as part of your role

- Accept that your credibility depends on doing the day job well

- Be deliberate in deciding when you handle the immediate and when you pass it to someone else

- Keep refining your approach to addressing recurring immediate issues

SEE A CRISIS AS AN OPPORTUNITY

A CRISIS CAN BE an opportunity to learn and to suggest how an organisation can handle immediate demands better.

The idea

Crises happen. When we pretend that they do not, we do so at our peril. Our domestic circumstances often prepare us for crises, especially if we are raising young children. It can be worth reflecting on who you have observed handling a crisis well and what you learnt from them. You might reflect on how you have handled a crisis in the past and what that taught you about both your preferences and the personal risks for you in a crisis.

A crisis can be an opportunity to assess what our instinctive reactions are and how well we work with others in a fast-moving and exposed situation. It can be a valuable learning process to volunteer to be part of addressing a crisis, so that you watch leaders at close range and observe how such situations are handled. Working with other people in a crisis situation will force you to be open to suggesting ideas and to responding quickly to the suggestions and direction of others. It can be like being part of a movie that is being played 'fast forward'.

Being part of handling a crisis situation can develop qualities in you that you are not expecting. You may be transferring into this new situation adaptability and resilience you have developed as a parent or as a community volunteer.

Being part of a team handling a crisis will enable you to observe how best you keep calm and keep focused on bringing your most effective contribution. Keeping calm might involve a combination of being clear on what matters most in a situation, and being detached enough to observe what is unfolding, and not be overwhelmed by either the emotions or the timescale.

Lin recognised that crises happened at the hospital, such as after an explosion at a nearby factory when a number of people needed surgery urgently. There were tried and tested procedures that she was responsible for implementing. Every crisis brought its pluses in terms of enabling staff to feel as if they were contributing fully to the work of the surgeons. Lin recognised that whenever parts of the hospital were under considerable pressure, there was always learning about qualities individuals possessed and about the need to keep reviewing and refining procedures that were not working as well as they could be.

In practice

- Accept that there will always be crises

- Think through how you will keep calm and be purposeful in a crisis

- See a crisis as an opportunity to contribute at your best and draw out the best in others

- Always look for the learning in a crisis both for yourself and in the way processes, procedures and expectations need to be refined

KNOW WHEN TO USE
THE LONG SCREWDRIVER

USING THE LONG SCREWDRIVER carefully is part of the repertoire of any manager or leader, but should be done selectively.

The idea

One senior leader I worked with received consistent criticism in his 360° feedback assessment that he used the long screwdriver too much. The leader accepted that most of the criticisms in the 360° feedback were fair. But he was clear that using the long screwdriver was an essential part of his leadership approach. He accepted that sometimes he could use the screwdriver more selectively, but he was not going to put the long screwdriver permanently back in the cupboard. This leader used a long screwdriver to follow up issues which he thought were particularly sensitive, and to assess on a dipstick basis how well the organisation was able to tackle some of the issues it was facing.

Critics might say that a leader using a long screwdriver is wasting their time and energy and taking away responsibility from others. Advocates might say that the ability to use a long screwdriver reinforces someone's knowledge about what is going on in an organisation and their capacity to assess how effective it is in dealing with a range of issues.

It is important to ration the number of occasions that you use the long screwdriver so that you do not distract yourself too much from your prime responsibilities, or let others conclude that all problems in the organisation will be solved by you. Perhaps you can ration yourself to two long screwdriver activities a month. It can be helpful for you to articulate why you are using a long screwdriver. For example, is it part of your continuous learning, or about seeking to understand what is happening within one part of the organisation?

Lin was uneasy about how one team was handling particular types of cases as they regularly seemed to be under major stress. She spent time talking to members of the team and observing them at work. She probed with questions about their comparative results and procedures compared with similar groups in other hospitals. Lin was polite but relentless.

Lin concluded that the level of mutual understanding amongst the team members was not as good as it should be. They could be easily thrown by the unexpected. She encouraged the team to work through how they had dealt with the unexpected in the past and how they would handle unexpected events going forward. She worked with them at procedural, emotional and behavioural levels. When she observed good progress beginning to happen, she withdrew.

In practice

- See the long screwdriver as part of your toolkit, but use it selectively

- Say why you are using the long screwdriver when you use it

- When you have made the progress you want to see happen, remove the long screwdriver quickly and see this as what you have done

- Watch if you get a reputation for using the long screwdriver too much

- Be conscious if some people want you to use the long screwdriver because it moves responsibility from them to you

ALWAYS BE ALERT TO CONSEQUENCES

WHATEVER ACTIONS YOU TAKE or are part of, always be alert to the consequences for other people and to potential next steps.

The idea

We finish a task and move on to the next one. We feel relieved or liberated that a task has been completed and want to hurry on to meet the next challenge. But what might be the consequences of the work we have done? How might it affect the lives of other people? How might the consequences feed into our description of the contribution we are making? Sometimes we can be so task-oriented that we see the completion of a task as its end rather than observing how the outcome of that task is changing lives and the expectations of others.

We might have participated in a project establishing a new community or church hall, but that is just the first stage. What matters now is how the facility is used for the good of the whole community. The process of maximising the benefit of the hall for the community is only just beginning.

Whatever action you take has consequences for your reputation. From the range of different interventions you make, a picture will develop in the minds of others about the distinctiveness of your contribution. If you are seen to intervene in a timely fashion, the consequence will be a reputation for intervening in the right way at the right time.

If you look stressed on more than a limited number of occasions the consequence will be a reputation that you are easily stressed. The law of consequences means that whatever behaviours you exhibit, your reputation will always be an exaggerated description of those behaviours. Positive behaviour can be turned over time into a strongly positive reputation, but just one or two moments of negative behaviour can have the immediate consequence of leading to a negative reputation.

Lin was conscious that whatever she said was taken seriously. If she questioned a particular activity the consequence was that this activity would be scrutinised thoroughly. She recognised that she could drop into conversations words of praise or questions that would be considered carefully. She knew that if she was sloppy in addressing an issue the consequence would be that others would be sloppy too.

Lin recognised that whenever she dealt with a short-term issue she had to think through what would be the consequences for the longer term. She asked herself regularly what would be the consequential behaviours of the consultant surgeons that would flow from the decisions she took.

In practice

- Always think through the longer-term consequences of actions you take in the short term

- Recognise that the comments you make and the questions you ask sow the seeds for subsequent substantive conversations

- Recognise that your attitude and approach will be mirrored by others so that the consequences of your approach will be felt more widely than you might anticipate

KNOW WHAT HELPS YOU TO THINK LONG TERM

WE ALL RECOGNISE THE importance of thinking long-term but we need prompts to ensure we do the necessary long-term thinking.

The idea

Some people long to be in the long-term thinking space, while others prefer to remain permanently sorting out the short term. Understanding our preferences and working with the grain of those preferences is a necessary step to getting the balance right between the short term and the long term.

It can be worth thinking through what captures our imagination about the longer term? What are long-term outcomes we particularly want to work towards? What will we and others feel is success in one or two years' time? Once we have clarity about desired outcomes it is easier to prioritise what to address in the short and medium term.

Steps that can help us think through longer-term issues might include talking with people who have dealt with similar issues before, and thinking through possibilities with others outside a formal meeting context. It might involve visiting other organisations and places where innovative approaches have led to constructive long-term outcomes and where we can have stimulating conversations about a range of possibilities.

It is unhelpful to view long-term thinking as something you do in spare moments. The risk is you then turn to longer-term subjects only when you are tired or when you feel guilty that you have not addressed them before. Allocating time to reflect on the longer term is crucial to success. How you spend that time depends on your preferences. For some people the best use of that time is in dialogue with others who are in similar worlds. For others the most stimulating approach is to talk with people in different worlds and addressing similar issues. For some what matters most is quiet self-reflection. For most of us it is a combination of activities in different proportions.

Lin recognised that there were fundamental issues to tackle about the use of consultant time and operating theatre space. If she tried to think through the issues in the margins of other things she got down-hearted. She visited some neighbouring hospitals that had addressed similar issues. She knew she had to allocate dedicated space with other interested people to work through the longer-term possibilities.

Lin worked co-operatively with a few thoughtful consultants, engaging them on what might be long-term options. She organised a couple of half-day workshops which enabled lively conversation about longer-term possibilities. She insisted on dedicated time being set aside for her and her team to think through options and test out scenarios.

In practice

- See addressing the long term as just as important as solving short-term problems

- Be clear what context enables you to think through long-term issues effectively

- Find conversation partners in people who are addressing or have addressed similar issues

- Accept that you and your team will be better equipped to think about the longer term on some days than on others, but when you are in the right frame of mind do grasp the opportunity wholeheartedly

WATCH IF THE URGENT DRIVES OUT THE IMPORTANT

THE URGENT NEEDS TO BE DONE but the important also needs to be tackled if success is to be built securely.

The idea

It can be helpful to spend preparatory time identifying what is urgent and what is important. The urgent and the important will overlap. Sometimes it is a matter of urgency to ask someone to take forward an important piece of action. Your action is to be clear where the responsibility lies, not to take on the action yourself.

A key question in balancing the urgent and the important is, 'What do I need to initiate, or what is the steer I need to give briefly that will allow the important to be addressed in an effective way?'

In any given week we will have a list of things we want to get done. Ensuring there is time allocated for the important when we are at our freshest is critical for success. It can be helpful to ration the amount of time for the urgent, which helps us sift which of the urgent tasks need to be done by us and which can be passed to others to address.

Rationing the amount of time we devote to dealing with e-mails can provide an effective sifting discipline. Our long-term wellbeing and success depend on us finding a way to deal with the urgent in a timely and discriminatory manner, whilst ensuring important short-term tasks are handled with proper due diligence. It can be helpful to decide at the start of a week what are the two or three important issues that you need to devote enough time to in order to move the action or thinking to the next phase.

Lin knew there would be urgent questions each day that needed addressing and that there were important issues she needed to set aside time to work on. Two members of staff were concerning her; she recognised that she needed to get to the root of the problems they were facing. There was a consultant who seemed overly critical about some of the procedures; Lin knew she had to understand her concerns and have a meeting with her about next steps. Neither of these conversations was urgent, but it was important that she addressed them in the next two or three weeks rather than leaving them to fester.

In practice

- Be clear what is urgent and what is important and how you deal with items in these two categories

- Recognise when you need to act urgently in order to give signals to others about their responsibilities and your expectations

- Define what important issues you need to address in the next couple of weeks and deal with them in a staged way so each issue gets your proper attention

- Be selective about which important issues need to be addressed first and be willing to park some issues until you have the time to devote to them

KEEP ABREAST OF THE THINKING OF OTHERS

KEEPING ABREAST of the thinking of others in the same sphere and in different spheres can help you keep sharp and adventurous.

The idea

When I coach a chief executive I will ask them how many other chief executives they are talking to in order to pool ideas and experiences. When I work with an emerging leader I encourage them to be in networks of other leaders at a similar stage in their careers so that they can share ideas and learn from each other's successes and failures.

It is always energising to be learning from someone else's journey and the innovations that have worked well for them. It can be helpful to talk with people from other countries to see how they have tackled similar issues. I periodically lead workshops at Regent College in Vancouver with leaders from a range of countries around the Pacific. We always have energetic debates as participants share their stories. When they work in small groups they come up with new ways of tackling problems they had previously found it difficult to solve. The resultant energy comes from thinking seriously about learning from others and experimenting with new approaches that have worked well elsewhere.

Keeping abreast of the thinking of others depends on setting aside time and energy. It means observing competitors carefully and seeing how they are changing the assumptions about what is possible. It is always worth putting yourself in the shoes of your client groups and reflecting on how their needs, preferences and expectations are changing. It may be that you need to update your approach so you are responding to current needs and preferences and not ones that are a few years out of date.

Lin recognised that she needed to update herself about the developing preferences of GPs and patient groups. She understood what the consultants wanted but needed to have a wider perspective about what other groups were looking for. She also needed a fuller appreciation of current thinking about good practice in similar hospitals. She organised a sequence of visits to meet the heads of GP practices and to a couple of hospitals. She did not return from these conversations with precise answers, but she became clearer about the questions that needed to be addressed more fully.

In practice

- Whose thinking is always stimulating for you? Can you spend more time with people who stretch your thinking?

- Whose approach might have moved on? How do you build a clearer appreciation of their current thinking?

- Who is working in a similar sphere as you with whom it would be good to catch up to share current thinking?

- Who has been writing articles or books in your area of interest? Can you set aside time to read what they have written?

- Recognise that you have thinking to offer others too, hence the importance of creating quality dialogue

KEEP ENGAGING WITH YOUR PEERS

Your peers can be an invaluable source of encouragement and constructive challenge. Do cultivate such relationships, in which you are committed to each other's success.

The idea

Ed Catmull in his book, *Creativity, Inc* (Random House, 2014), tells the story of Pixar Animation Studios as it grew its success. His book includes a key chapter, entitled 'Honesty and Candour', in which he describes the 'Braintrust' that operated within the organisation. Every director had to bring their films as they developed at different stages to the Braintrust, which provided a forum for robust peer review.

Catmull writes: 'Each of the participants focused on the film at hand and not on some hidden agenda. They argued, sometimes heatedly, but always about the project. They were not motivated by the kind of things – getting credit for an idea, pleasing their supervisors, winning a point just to say you did – that too often lurk beneath the surface of work-related interactions.'

The Braintrust members saw each other as peers. The passionate opinions expressed in Braintrust meetings were never taken personally because everyone knew that they were directed at solving problems. Largely because of that trust and mutual respect, the Braintrust's problem-solving powers were immense. Members tested weak points and made suggestions, but it was up to each film's director to settle on a path forward. Catmull describes the movies steadily improving with each iteration.

The Braintrust example is an exemplar of mutual challenge by peers bringing high standards, candour and openness, but then leaving it to the individual responsible for a project to decide how to apply the feedback.

Lin always benefited from meeting with peers in similar hospitals. She set up a learning set involving five peers, with the members taking turns to present issues that they were addressing and seek feedback from the others. Initially participants were hesitant to criticise each other's initiatives, but their confidence in each other grew stronger. They began to be increasingly robust with each other when they had concerns about the implications of steps colleagues were taking. They took turns to be in the 'hot seat' and always benefited from the rigorous conversation that ensued.

In practice

- How might Braintrust-type ideas apply in your work area?

- What type of learning set might you set up with people in similar roles where you can learn from each other's experience?

- Who are the peers you relate best to? Can you set up mutual peer support arrangements on the basis that you are committed to each other's success?

AVOID GETTING ENTRAPPED BY THE LATEST FASHIONABLE THINKING

IT IS ALWAYS WORTH reflecting on whatever is the latest fashionable thinking – without being entrapped by it.

The idea

There are always buzzwords about management and leadership that are in vogue for a period. For a while the rhetoric was about vision and values, then the language of being an authentic leader became fashionable. Mindfulness has been popular for a couple of years.

All such ideas are valuable as part of a wider picture, but too much stress on one concept can mean you end up talking a language that others find theoretical and alienating. The overuse of one word can be off-putting to others, especially if it is a word like 'systemic' which sounds theoretical but simply means looking at the whole system.

If the leader of your organisation is seeking to apply a particular concept it is worth going with the grain of that notion so you understand how you can best contribute. If, for example, the leader is talking about 'distributed leadership', it is worth being clear what they mean by that phrase. It may mean no more than effective delegation of responsibilities.

Once you are clear what the leader is intending, you can create your own practical application of that concept in your part of the organisation. You can be describing your intent through examples that are meaningful for your staff and colleagues. You can then illustrate how you are implementing the boss's expectations without having to use the same buzzword in every other sentence. In this way you are focusing on the reality of the changes you are seeking to implement without being restricted to the constant repetition of the favoured buzzword.

Lin always knew when the hospital chief executive had been on a course as he would return energised with a new pet theory. The chief executive would talk enthusiastically and encourage people to read a particular book or article. Lin had trained herself to note two or three key points from what the chief executive was saying, and then assess where those points were relevant in her area within the hospital.

The chief executive always had good things to say and drew wisely from what she had learnt in other places. Lin was conscious that she must not be overwhelmed by the chief executive's enthusiasm. What worked for Lin was identifying two or three key points and building those points in her own words into her narrative, describing where she was seeking to lead her part of the organisation over the next few weeks.

In practice

- Keep absorbing new ideas and approaches

- See each new idea as adding to your repertoire rather than taking over from the last idea

- Beware if you begin to use theoretical words in a way your hearers do not understand

- Recognise when a word or concept has gone out of fashion and then only use it selectively

- If it sounds complicated start again and say what you want to say simply and clearly

BE READY TO HAND OVER THE SHORT TERM TO OTHERS

MAKING SURE YOU keep handing over responsibilities to others gives you the space to develop new ideas and widen your influence.

The idea

The good leader is for ever developing an idea, creating a sense of direction, building a team to take forward the idea and then letting that team take it from there. The experienced leader will then keep their distance and check in from time to time on the progress.

An effective leader will have appointed key lieutenants who can take forward day-to-day business, releasing them to focus on steering, handling the most difficult decisions and addressing the longer term. Good lieutenants who are going to thrive need resilience and sound judgement, plus a willingness to take on significant responsibility. The effective leader will take time and care in making such appointments, and then act as a mentor to the appointees to help grow their confidence and effectiveness.

There is a risk that we are reluctant to hand the lead to others as we recognise that we will still be accountable for the success of the enterprise. But it is only as we hand over responsibility that we fully develop others and create space to take forward wider learning and make the fuller contribution we want to make.

It might be worth having a discipline of deciding every month to hand over to others three areas where you have been previously in the lead. You are not abdicating your accountability; you are using your role and influence to help ensure that the activities continue to be led successfully. Increasingly the aim might be to be seen as a mentor, advisor and strategic contributor rather than as the leader of individual projects.

Lin wanted to see as many of her people promoted as possible. The best way to ensure this was to give them clear responsibility leading to successful outcomes. Both she and the individual leaders then got the credit for good results.

Sometimes Lin's boss would question her about why she had given responsibility to a more junior member of staff and not been in the lead herself. Lin recognised when she was likely to be asked this question and always had a clear rationale and was able to share evidence about the progress of those people to whom she had delegated responsibility. She recognised that she did not always get the delegation right. Periodically someone would let her down. But overall identifying people who were ready to take responsibility and then giving them responsibility provided a formula that worked for her.

In practice

- Consider having a notional target about how many tasks you can hand to others over the next month

- See yourself as someone who steers, mentors and develops people, not as someone who always does everything yourself

- Build an understanding with your boss that handing on responsibility and developing the next level of staff is central to your job

- Be ready with a persuasive narrative when your boss questions you about the way you hand over responsibility

SECTION H
SUSTAIN THE SUCCESS

71 ENSURING SUSTAINED SUCCESS

SUCCESS IS NOT ABOUT one victory; it is about sustaining yourself through many different phases.

The idea

Albert Johanneson was the first black football player to play in an English FA Cup Final at Wembley in 1965. He was a brilliant dribbler but subsequently did not hold his place in the Leeds United team and was soon playing in a lower division before leaving football altogether. He was not the first footballer to be initially successful and then suffer a drop in form linked with declining confidence and drinking more alcohol than was good for him.

Too much success too early can elate us and make us believe that we are invincible. When the next success is more elusive our confidence can collapse. We build our long-term resolve more effectively if we have a sequence of small successes which reinforce our capabilities without allowing success to 'go to our head'.

When we are successful we need people around us who will help us recognise why we have been successful, and enable us to build on that success in a measured and realistic way. A good coach of a youth sports team is both encouraging and demanding of the players. They praise what the players do well in order to reinforce their capabilities, but are for ever stretching them and enabling them to progress incrementally to even higher standards of attainment.

The good athlete recognises that sustaining success requires physical training and mental resolve, alongside maintaining emotional equilibrium.

Paul was head of the sixth form at a secondary school where the examination results had been getting consistently better. He had taken over from an outstanding head of the sixth form and was apprehensive about whether he could bring the same level of leadership as his predecessor. He recognised that success resulted from the dedicated hard work of many teachers. It was through sustaining his teachers that good examination results would be maintained. Paul spent a lot of time in his new role getting to know the teachers better and learning how to encourage and motivate them effectively.

In practice

- Remember what sustained you after your first success and kept you striving for subsequent successes

- When people you work with are successful, acknowledge their success as a step towards whatever they might want to do in the longer term

- Enable individuals and teams to enjoy success and see how they can build on that success

- Enable others to focus on how they sustain their energy and commitment in the fallow period following a success

72 ONE LAYER OF BRICKS AT A TIME

A BUILDING IS STABLE because it is constructed one layer of bricks at a time.

The idea

Young children love to build a tower by putting one brick on top of another brick and then laugh as they push the unstable tower over. The youngster's tower had grown tall quickly, but fell even faster when given a gentle nudge.

After a while the youngster learns to build a stronger wall by placing bricks one at a time alongside each other, and then placing another layer of bricks which are not immediately on top of the previous bricks. The youngster learns that this robust wall is much harder to demolish than the original tall pile of bricks placed one immediately on top of the other.

Effective learning proceeds one layer at a time. We practise the skill of chairing small meetings and then gradually move up to chairing larger meetings. We feel relaxed giving a presentation to six people and then build on that experience so we are presenting to 20 people, and then 60 people, and then 150 people.

We are taught by good mentors and bosses to take one step at a time and to see progress as building successive layers of bricks, with each layer being robust and serving as the sound basis for a further layer of bricks.

As we build our experience and credibility, equal care needs to be put into each stage of our development, so we build effectively this month on what we did last month.

Paul recalled how he had built the support and commitment of his people when leading the science department. He grew their commitment through respecting their professionalism and drawing them into decisions about next steps. Paul knew that when he became head of the sixth form he already had a lot of credibility because of the way he had led the science department. He adopted a similar approach of building up people's confidence and goodwill, whilst stretching them to think further about how they wanted to continue to develop their professionalism and widen their contribution.

In practice

- Recall how you have built your credibility and success one layer at a time

- Anticipate how you are going to use the same approach to build further layers of effectiveness into your contribution as a leader

- Consider how best you develop the confidence and competence of those working with you one layer at a time so you are developing and sustaining the next generation of leaders

73 USE RESILIENT MORTAR

THE QUALITY OF THE MORTAR is crucial if the bricks are to stay in place and a building is to be robust.

The idea

If the mortar used in constructing a brick building is poor and begins to disintegrate, the building can quickly become unstable. Good-quality mortar enables bricks to be gripped together, thereby enabling a wall to stand up effectively to battering from wind, rain and time.

The strength of a wall depends not only on the quality of the bricks, but on the mortar holding the bricks together. If a wall is just bricks with no mortar it will be unstable. The interleaving layers of mortar give the wall its strength and resilience. The bricks and the mortar act together as a unit and jointly create a strong wall. If the wall is just mortar with no bricks it will be impossible to build a sturdy, attractive wall.

Perhaps the mortar is like the shared values of a team working together, or a shared history that provides a sense of identity, or a common purpose. Participants recognise that the bricks need to be held together in a way that ensures strength in the whole wall. The strength might come from handling issues such as winds of change or gales that seek to destroy.

Paul developed a sense of shared endeavour involving all the staff teaching in the sixth form through building a set of expectations one layer at a time. Each time he built a layer he ensured that the mortar that held each layer together was about shared values and mutual respect. He then reinforced constructive ways of working co-operatively together. He recognised that the mortar that held the bricks together was just as important as each brick to ultimate success.

In practice

- When you have been part of a successful team, what was the mortar that held the team together?

- As you build successful ventures going forward, what do you see as the mortar that will hold the bricks together?

- How best do you ensure that others see the mortar as important in the way it holds people together and provides a set of shared values and combined endeavour?

74 ENSURE YOU BUILD UPWARDS

WE NEED TO CHECK periodically that we are building in the direction we originally intended.

The idea

A lot of thought and creative thinking goes into the preparation of a plan for building a home extension, but once the plan has been approved by the relevant government authority it becomes a set of constraints.

Our enthusiasm and curiosity may encourage us to keep developing a range of different ideas that are only tangentially linked to one another. This creative phase can be stimulating and worthwhile, but once a plan has been shaped, agreement reached and funding secured, the task is to construct the building to the required specification. The moment for lateral thinking about design has passed; what is needed now is a staged and disciplined approach that leads to a building constructed according to plan and in line with regulations.

There are times as we seek to build success when we need to proceed according to a clear plan. Major experimentation is put on hold as we seek to make good progress moving a project forward or delivering results. We have timescales to adhere to and quality standards to meet. This is the moment to focus on agreed action and not be distracted. There are phases when delivery is all-important. What matters is recognising those moments and not being deflected by the extraneous or by your curiosity.

Paul had spent many hours talking with those teaching in the sixth form about how they might develop the curriculum offer. After this lengthy consultation period decisions were made about reshaping the curriculum. Now was the moment when Paul needed to ensure that the edifice of the sixth form curriculum was built effectively and on time. This was the season for turning aspirations into clear plans and agreed next steps. Paul needed to be persistent with some people about building clearly on agreements reached in order to ensure that the overall curriculum was constructed soundly and visibly.

In practice

- Be clear when you move from design to construction

- Give credit to those who have contributed in the design period, but then expect them to stick to agreed plans

- Ensure the right constraints are in place so that progress is systematic and in the agreed direction

- Be quick to identify in advance the issues that can impede next steps or bring action to a halt

75 WATCH FOR SUBSIDENCE

WHEN YOU ARE LOOKING UPWARDS you need to be alert to what might be sinking beneath you.

The idea

The first signs of subsidence can be some hairline cracks that are barely visible. We dismiss the cracks as inevitable. It is only when the cracks become markedly bigger or when water begins to seep into the building that we realise that there is a significant problem.

We view subsidence as an unhelpful surprise. Often the causes of likely subsidence are invisible to the trained eye. The surveyor will be looking for indications that subsidence might be a problem and assessing the degree of risk with care.

When we are taking forward a project or building a new organisation we need to reflect on what might be happening underneath the surface. The foundations for our plans might not be as strong and secure as we had anticipated. Some of our assumptions about the support of others may be less robust than we had hoped.

It is worth reflecting on what are the potential risks of subsidence. How can we anticipate them and then ameliorate them?

Drawing in experts can allow the risk of subsidence to be identified. On other occasions subsidence just happens without warning. When the unexpected happens and the bottom falls out of our plans, what matters is the combination of careful analysis of the new situation and then a shared resolve to address next steps effectively.

Paul was conscious that no matter how carefully he constructed the edifice of the new sixth form curriculum, there would be some cracks and some subsidence. One teacher fell ill and needed time off. Another teacher lacked the confidence to develop her part of the curriculum. Paul had included some contingency provision, but this was being stretched as three teachers were unable to fulfil their commitments. He quickly recruited a couple of teachers on short-term contracts who could both contribute to curriculum development and teach parts of the curriculum well. He was concerned that he had not anticipated the problems as fully as he might have done, but was pleased with the contingency arrangements now in place.

In practice

- Look out for the cracks that might appear in projects or organisations you are leading

- Look carefully at the risks to assess what likelihood there might be of subsidence

- Be prepared to act quickly and decisively if cracks appear or subsidence begins to happen

- Do not waste time blaming yourself if subsidence happens unexpectedly

KNOW WHEN YOU NEED UNDERPINNING

THERE ARE TIMES WHEN you need a lot of support. Be willing to accept support graciously that is given generously.

The idea

Sometimes we feel strong, independent and able to handle any task thrown at us. We thrive in such moments when we feel that anything is possible and every problem solvable.

In such moments we might not fully appreciate how much we depend on others for practical and emotional support. Someone is ensuring that the IT system is working, and that the heating or air-conditioning is operating effectively in the building in which you are sitting. A colleague has provided tea and coffee, and someone else might have reminded you about a meeting you had forgotten.

Behind every successful woman or man there are normally others who expend and commit time and energy being supportive. Perhaps it is a hard-working spouse who looks after day-to-day household needs or who provides most of the family income. Perhaps it is a long-suffering administrative assistant who organises the diary and meeting papers. The risk is that the busy manager or leader takes for granted those who spend time and energy unobtrusively supporting them.

If a building's foundations begin to move, underpinning is necessary to secure the foundations and ensure the physical stability of the building. Sometimes the foundations we have relied on for a long period begin to shift and similarly need underpinning. This may be a moment when we need to draw on the resources of others to strengthen our resilience and the foundations on which we build.

Paul recognised that he had embarked on a sequence of major changes which at times did not feel as secure and stable as he had hoped. He relied on his deputy, Sue, more than he perhaps appreciated. He recognised that in this next phase, when he wanted to ensure the foundations for the next steps were strong and secure, he needed Sue's active support. He spent more time with Sue sharing his thoughts and drawing out her practical ideas. He affirmed her contribution to the next stages and recognised that she was providing valuable underpinning for what they were seeking to deliver.

In practice

- Whose contribution underpins what you do now?

- How can you affirm those people who underpin what you do?

- What underpinning will you need in the future, and how best do you prepare for that?

- How willing are you to be supported by others and not rely purely on your own capabilities and independence?

USE A PLUMB LINE

USING A PLUMB LINE ENABLES YOU to assess whether a building is being constructed vertically, so that it is structurally stable and will not collapse.

The idea

When a wall is being built it is crucial to have external validation that it is being built vertically, with the bricks lying horizontally. A plumb line assesses whether a wall is vertical, with a spirit level enabling you to assess whether the layers of bricks are horizontal. As we build a wall we may be standing so close to it that we cannot readily identify if the bricks have been laid with clear vertical lines and in horizontal layers. The plumb line and spirit level tell us the truth; they do not lie or distort the facts.

When we build a set of intentions for the future of an organisation, we need independent validation about the integrity of what we are doing. We are seeking to build an organisation that complies with specified requirements and agreed values, but it can be helpful if there is an independent perspective.

A plumb line is not used once and then forgotten; it is used on a regular basis as the building is being constructed. When I was responsible for major projects as a Finance Director, I ensured there were regular health-checks of projects to assess whether progress was consistent with the requirements. This provided a valuable discipline and gave useful early warning of problems. Regular health-checks provided a plumb line to assess the on-going success of projects.

Paul had periodic conversations with a former colleague who had become head of the sixth form in a secondary school 20 miles away. The two sixth forms were not in competition because of geographical separation. The two former colleagues decided that they could act as a plumb line for each other. Twice a year they spent a couple of days in the other's school talking to teachers individually, sitting in on meetings and looking at curriculum plans and timetables. Following an intensive two days, Paul knew that his colleague would be able to give him helpful reflections on whether the curriculum and ethos of the sixth form were consistent with the espoused intentions and values.

In practice

- How open are you to testing what you are building using a plumb line?

- What type of external health-check or verification do you find is most accurate and helpful for you?

- How best do you ensure that you have an open mind when you receive external feedback?

TEST THE STRENGTH

It is important to test the strength of any project or plan to see if it is robust.

The idea

When you build a shed you want it to withstand the wind and the rain. The shed might look attractive, but if it is unstable or wobbly it is unlikely to survive inclement weather. When you build a shed you probably push it hard to see if the corners are robust; you are likely to reinforce the corners if the shed is not as sound as you want.

When I constructed a set of bunks from a kit when the children were small, the wooden slats did not appear very strong and one snapped as I pushed it gently. The hardware store accepted that the slats were not robust and provided me with a set of thicker slats that were robust enough to cope with an energetic nine-year-old.

Whatever we build, we need to be able to test its strength. If we are building a team or organisation we need to ensure that it includes the right mix of competences and is able to be resilient in times of external pressure.

When we are building our own future we need to be able to test the strength of the capabilities we are putting together. Building the right level of strength and resilience into our aspirations may be about appropriate further education and training. It can be about developing skills and practising those skills in a variety of situations. It can mean thinking through how we develop our personal influence and impact, and then practising those skills in a range of different contexts.

As we develop the resolve to make a success of whatever sphere we are in, we will hopefully be developing the strength of that resolve. Do disappointments strengthen that resolve or dampen our enthusiasm? If strength and resolve still exist after a sequence of disappointments we are likely to find that our sustainability has increased.

Paul thought that the remodelled expectations within the sixth form about its curriculum and ways of working were firmly in the right direction. It was fine to be talking positively about the changes but what mattered was what students decided. He and Sue, his deputy, ran an information campaign with 15-year-olds in the school. In previous years a number had left to go to a sixth form college. Paul's intent was to capture the imagination of these 15-year-olds so that they went into the school's sixth form. He and Sue had to create a coherent and persuasive story about the subject mix and the resulting university options. Paul was confident that he was ready to test the market.

In practice

- How robust are your intentions for the future in terms of building the right qualifications, credibility and experience?

- How open are you to assessing the strength of your aspirations by testing them out in safe environments?

- How open are you to others pushing you hard to test out the robustness of your thinking about the future?

79 USE QUALITY MATERIALS

WHEN WE USE quality materials and craftsmanship positive outcomes are much more likely to be sustained.

The idea

How often have we regretted using poor materials? The mortar between the paving stones begins to break up after three or four years because we skimped on using the best materials. The nails begin to go rusty in the shed because we bought the cheapest ones. The table begins to creak because the joints were not fitted perfectly as we had rushed to finish the job late one afternoon.

Investment in quality materials and good craftsmanship is rarely wasted when constructing a building which you want to have a long life. As you build an organisation it is worth asking if you are investing enough time and energy in recruiting the right people, building robust procedures and ensuring the reinforcement of the right attitudes and positive behaviours. If you have any doubts in your answers to these questions it is worth thinking again about the nature and quality of the investment you are making.

As you reflect on building the next steps in your career it is worth thinking about how you are investing in yourself, and whether you are investing in the right quality of education, training and practical experience. Are you building the right quality of people around you to help ensure strength and depth in what you are seeking to build?

Paul recognised that building an effective sixth form curriculum depended on investing in new staff, upskilling existing staff and ensuring up-to-date IT. He was clear that he must not go for second best when recruiting new people. He set up workshops with experienced facilitators to enable the existing staff to think through how they were going to update their teaching methods for a new generation of students. He worked with three members of the sixth form plus the head of IT to develop a more accessible lesson planning program. He was relentless in focusing on the quality and sustainability of the systems he introduced.

In practice

- When have you been tempted to accept second best in terms of materials and what were the results?

- How do you assess your level of investment in the right quality of people and materials without being unnecessarily extravagant?

- As you build the next steps in your career, what are the quality materials you would do well to invest in?

80 BE WILLING TO DEMOLISH A BUILDING

SOMETIMES THE BEST THING TO DO IS to demolish a building and start again.

The idea

Sometimes refurbishment and renewal creates an outcome that is as good as new. On other occasions a building needs to be demolished and the construction started again. Perhaps demolition leaves the foundation intact, and it continues to provide a firm basis for the new building. On other occasions it is the foundation that has been part of the problem; the removal of the foundation becomes an essential prerequisite before a new building can be constructed that can withstand the elements.

After an earthquake or typhoon the remains of a destroyed structure have to be removed completely before there is any point in starting new construction. When building an organisation we sometimes have to go back to the start and reassess why an organisation exists at all and what are its objectives. Sometimes the foundations have to be reconstructed and the organisation repopulated with new people who do not bring historic baggage and can look at issues anew.

When you are building your future there are times when it is right to start again. After doing an undergraduate degree in geography I did a postgraduate master's degree in traffic engineering and planning. Part way through this course I realised that a career in traffic engineering and planning was not for me. I chose to complete the master's degree while exploring other possible career avenues. I had invested time and money in the course and had to accept that it was leading nowhere. What mattered was being open to start again and not regretting taking this master's degree.

Paul observed that one department had consistently poor examination results. His predecessor had not tackled this problem head on. Paul knew that he could not ignore this poor department as it was affecting the reputation of the overall sixth form. His options were either to strengthen the department or close it down. He persuaded a member of staff to retire early and invested in some intensive updating for the other member of staff. He recruited a new staff member who brought energy to the department. He was glad he had taken decisive action, even though it led to some personal conflict.

In practice

- How willing are you to demolish something you have constructed if it is not fully fit for purpose?

- In what areas of your life do you need to demolish an edifice you have built which is now irrelevant or unused?

- How do you prepare yourself emotionally to demolish and rebuild?

- How best can you demolish a building that you and others have constructed while keeping the consequential pain to a minimum?

SECTION I
GROW TEAM SUCCESS

WHAT ARE THE EXPECTATIONS OF OTHERS ABOUT THE TEAM?

UNDERSTANDING THE EXPECTATIONS of key stakeholders is a first step in building team success.

The idea

This section assumes you are responsible for a team and want to ensure it is successful and regarded as successful. The first step is clarity about the expectations of those who set up the team. Does the team have a clear remit and timescale with specific outcomes that will either be achieved or not? Are the expectations specific in terms of how a team develops an approach to address a problem?

There may be a range of expectations from customers or stakeholders, with some being vague and unsaid, and others declared at every available opportunity. Sometimes the expectations have to be dampened down and put onto a more realistic timescale. On other occasions it is necessary to draw out from different people with an interest what success would look like.

When a team has been set up it is always worth the team leader talking with a range of different people to establish what their expectations are and on what timescale. This gives the team leader the opportunity to clarify what are reasonable expectations and use that understanding as the basis for the future programme of work.

Mustaq was the chief administrative officer at a growing university and was leading a team addressing how to handle the planned expansion of the university. There were varied views about the type of expansion, in what subjects, full-time or part-time students, and under what timescale. Mustaq recognised the strongly held views of the academics but also understood the realism brought by the finance director and the estates director.

Mustaq knew he had to bring key people in the room together to build a set of expectations that would be both ambitious and realistic. He recognised he needed to be relentless in ensuring that there was proper debate about the different expectations, with a set of conclusions reached and accepted as achievable on an agreed timescale.

In practice

- What are the expectations of those who set up the team you are leading?

- How varied are the expectations of those with an interest in the work of the team, such as clients, customers and staff?

- What are the common themes in the expectations of the participants in the team, and how acute are the differences between them?

- How best do you surface different expectations and ensure thoughtful consideration of next steps?

WHAT ARE YOUR SOURCES OF INFLUENCE?

WHEN LEADING A TEAM it is worth being clear what are your formal, informal and reputational sources of influence over the team's success.

The idea

Your formal influence comes from your status and rank within an organisation, together with the authority given to you and your team by those with legal and financial accountability. Your informal influence comes from the way you communicate and your networks within and outside the organisation. Your reputational influence comes from your credibility, your track record and how effective you are perceived to be.

In any given situation your level of influence flows from the combination of these three sources. The perception of your team is shaped by the influence you are able to have as team leader. Over time the credibility and impact of the whole team will be noticed and you will continue to cast a shadow over its reputation, for good or ill.

Your success in leading a team depends on using these different sources of influence well. You may want to focus on informal influence as a means of building goodwill and support and hold your formal influence in the background.

Your reputational influence may need updating. For example, if your reputation is that you can be disorganised it will be important to demonstrate that the team you are setting up will be operating within a clear process and timescale. If your reputation is for being highly structured, you might want to be having informal conversations to demonstrate your openness to learning and your adaptability of approach.

Mustaq's background was in project management and therefore he liked structured processes. He built credibility through putting in place effective systems that worked. He also recognised that informal links made it easier for processes to run effectively. He was conscious that he could sometimes over-rely on process and was determined when setting up this team that he developed an open and co-operative working relationship with the different interests.

In practice

- In your current role how much of your influence flows from each of the three sources – formal, informal and reputational?

- In any team you lead how do you seek to balance formal and informal influence?

- What is your natural preference about applying formal and informal influencing approaches?

- What do you notice about differences in the way you influence within the team you are leading and outside it?

WHAT CAN BE BEST DONE AS A TEAM?

CAREFUL THOUGHT ABOUT WHAT can be best done by individuals and what can be done more effectively by a team is always beneficial.

The idea

The success of the long-distance cyclist depends on how they work with other members of their team. As they switch the lead between members of the team they are conserving each other's energy and maximising the prospect of overall success. The good cycling team will understand the varying capabilities of team members, recognising who is the fastest on the flat stretches and who climbs hills most effectively.

In any team some tasks are best carried out individually, for example the accountant or lawyer giving specific professional consideration and advice. On other issues what is needed is a combination of perspectives, with practical ideas emanating from the interaction of different team members.

Creativity within a team may be at its best when difficult issues are being wrestled with from different perspectives, and when the discussion of long-term possibilities seeks to draw on the range of experiences and ideas within the team.

A successful team will be drawing on the best of what individuals can do and on stimulating interaction and exchange between members. The task of the team leader is to get the best out of both the individuals and the extra dimension that results from team interaction.

Mustaq was clear that there were specific pieces of analysis that needed to be done by individual team members. He was conscious that he had a group of strong-minded people whom he needed to ensure operated successfully together, understanding each other's concerns and building on each other's ideas.

Mustaq organised a three-hour workshop in which team members were encouraged to be open about their preferred ways of working, how they wanted to contribute to the team and what they wanted from team members to draw the best from them. This led to open discussion about what they could most effectively do as individuals and what they thought they could best do as a team. They agreed on the frequency of their meetings and the format to adopt for the more reflective conversations, where sitting around a formal central table would be banned.

In practice

- Share examples of teams that have been successful, reflecting on the reasons for their success

- Be open about your own preferences about when you work best as an individual and when as part of a team

- Invite team members to talk of their own preferences and hopes for how the team is going to work effectively together going forward

- Encourage open discussion about the relationship between the success of the team and how it has been working together

- Ensure success is marked and celebrated when it flows from good-quality team interaction or co-operation

WHEN IS IT A TEAM RESPONSIBILITY AND NOT YOUR RESPONSIBILITY ALONE?

As TEAM LEADER you are ultimately accountable, but responsibility is shared by the whole team and is not yours to bear alone.

The idea

As a team leader you carry ultimate accountability. As a consequence you are likely to feel a burden of responsibility for each part of the team's work. Taking responsibility firmly on your shoulders is dutiful and conscientious but may not be entirely helpful.

Members of a long-distance cycling team have a strong sense of responsibility to one another and to the overall success of the team. Any well-functioning team will have a strong sense of mutual accountability.

It can be helpful for a team to discuss on a regular basis what are the individual responsibilities and what is the overall team responsibility to which everyone is committed. There is likely to be a shared responsibility for good-quality contributions to the team, thoughtful interaction, and the way conclusions are arrived at and followed up, coupled with a responsibility to support the overall team objectives.

As team leader there will be moments when you need to remind the team that they have committed themselves to certain standards and outcomes, and that it is everyone's responsibility to ensure these are delivered. There will be moments when it is important to say this explicitly and not just assume that people will follow previous agreements.

Mustaq was concerned that the estates director was so focused on the quality of pieces of building work that the overriding purpose of admitting more students tended to take second place. Mustaq respected his colleague's commitment to building standards but knew he needed to persuade his colleague that the student number increase was the prime objective rather than the best possible quality buildings.

Mustaq did not want to embarrass his colleague by pressing this point too strongly in the team meetings. He deliberately spent an hour with this colleague, one-to-one, working this issue through and being frank about his concerns. The colleague recognised the point and accepted their team responsibility.

In practice

- Be explicit about individual responsibilities and team responsibilities

- Get the team to talk through how it is going to ensure it takes its overall responsibilities seriously

- When you feel as if people are putting team responsibilities back onto you, be open in talking within the team about the balance between team and individual responsibilities

- Be explicit when something is your responsibility and be fully accountable for it

- Be fulsome in acknowledging when a team has taken forward its responsibilities successfully

WHEN DO YOU ENSURE THE CREDIT GOES TO OTHERS?

ENSURING CREDIT GOES TO OTHERS enhances rather than diminishes your reputation.

The idea

There is a risk, if you think your aim is to build your own success, that you will want the credit always to go to you. In fact, it is in your interest in many cases for credit to go to others rather than yourself. You want the team to do well and to be seen to do well. Ensuring that the team gets the credit builds your reputation as someone who can lead and motivate a team.

If you want to build up the support of other people in your organisation the more you can ensure that they get full credit for the contribution they have made and the outcomes they have delivered, the greater the likelihood of their contributing constructively to future initiatives that you are involved in.

Talking about the positive contribution that members of your team are making in wider discussions reinforces their reputation and credibility, provided the praise is based on reality and is not overdone. Exaggerated praise of your team members will ring false and can damage the seriousness with which your views are taken.

There are moments when it is important that your leadership contribution is recognised. In performance appraisals and in your CV it is appropriate to claim full credit for the impact of your leadership of a team's work. In interview-type situations you will want to give full credit to your team and be explicit about your contribution. Most of the time you will want to give credit to others, while demonstrating that you take your team leadership responsibilities seriously.

Mustaq was seeking to build the commitment of his team members to the major project. He deliberately gave them a lot of credit for the quality of their individual contributions and the progress they were beginning to make. He did not seek to take credit for what he was doing. He knew that he would be judged by the success of the whole project. He knew the University Vice-Chancellor would be observing the level of commitment of the team members. Mustaq's success in the short term depended on him being seen to have the full commitment of all the function heads who were members of the team.

In practice

- How readily do you give credit to other people?

- How willing are you to subordinate your desire for acknowledgement to the greater good of the overall endeavour?

- What are some key moments where you would want to ensure you get appropriate credit for the leadership you have been bringing?

- How best do you ensure the balance between giving credit to other people and ensuring you get appropriate credit when it comes to performance assessment or applying for other roles?

HOW DO YOU KEEP A TEAM FRESH AND ALERT?

OVER TIME, a team may develop a routine and become uninspiring to others, hence the importance of keeping the team fresh and alert.

The idea

I used to observe analysts giving presentations to a committee with regulatory responsibilities and then I would give feedback to the presenters. This committee sat around a formal table looking severe. Each of them would have a laptop open, with the screen acting as a barrier between them and others in the room. Each presenter came in at the start of their item to this large room and was expected to be charming, persuasive and able to answer any question. The formal layout of the room was off-putting, the tone was sombre, and comments were often abrupt. The committee members did not exude a lively welcome or engage in fresh debate. People were invariably apprehensive about giving a presentation to them.

A team needs to be deliberate about how it keeps fresh and alert. A good barometer is the views of those joining the committee for an item and having to present to it. The tone of the welcome, the shape of the room, the removal of unnecessary barriers, and the interest shown in the discussion all have a part to play. Nothing kills freshness more than a long Powerpoint presentation. What matters in keeping any team fresh is the sharing of examples and stories which feed the imagination about what is possible going forward.

Mustaq recognised that some of his team members could be ultra-cautious and hide behind process. He decided his team should meet in different places, have varied types of agendas, pay a visit to a university that was increasing its student numbers radically, and meet together informally as well as formally. Mustaq deliberately moved away from a formula of always operating in plenary discussions; in meetings they would sometimes talk in twos and threes on specific subjects and share their conclusions.

In practice

- When do you observe a team being at its most alert and fresh, and what differentiates such situations from occasions when a team looks flat?

- What helps you be alert and fresh in the way you lead a team?

- What type of conversation can you have with team members about how best you help keep the team fresh and alert?

- How bold are you willing to be in altering the usual routines within your organisation through using different venues, approaches and mixing small-group and plenary conversations?

HOW DO YOU ENABLE A TEAM TO HANDLE CONFLICT WELL?

ANY TEAM THAT IS ABLE to surface and handle conflict well is likely to be more effective than a team that suppresses conflict.

The idea

Our natural assumption is to think of conflict as bad and harmony as good. The most successful teams are open about differences of opinion, frank in handling conflict and generous in moving on from conflict into a shared purpose. When tackling a demanding issue some conflict is almost inevitable. It is far better that conflict is surfaced in a structured way rather than allowed to fester.

Success only comes for a team when areas of conflict have been fully explored and an accommodation reached about how next steps are to be tackled in a way that brings participants together instead of driving them apart.

If there is conflict about a desired outcome the team leader has a responsibility to be clear about expectations so there is no ambiguity about outcomes. If a conflict is about underlying values or behaviours there can be a need to tease out what people understand as key values and how they might be applied or misunderstood. If the conflict is about ways of working there needs to be frank conversation about why it is in the team's interest to find better ways of working together.

The skilful team leader will ensure that discussion about handling conflict is about issues and not personalities. Depersonalising an issue is a key step so that the consideration is about how to tackle an issue and not about impugning the integrity of a colleague.

Mustaq arranged an early conversation about some areas of potential disagreement. Naming these areas and writing them on a flipchart allowed participants to talk openly about how substantive these points of difference might be and the extent to which they might get in the way of open and constructive conversation.

Because team members had discussed how they would handle these types of potential disagreements, they were in a much better position to address them when they arose. For example, there was a marked difference of view about how important participants felt student support was compared with academic provision. They recognised as a team that there were strongly different views on this and worked out how they would assess the relative levels of different types of resource provision as student numbers grew.

In practice

- Ask people to share how they have handled conflict effectively in previous teams

- Set aside time for a team to work through how they are going to handle potential conflict in the future

- Invite people to name potential areas of conflict and work through an agreed strategy for dealing with these areas

- Encourage participants to consider that conflict is healthy and best not suppressed

- Always seek to depersonalise conflict

HOW BEST DO YOU INVEST IN COLLEAGUES?

THE MORE YOU INVEST in your colleagues the more you build supporters who will contribute to the success of ventures you are part of.

The idea

The more you invest time and energy in your colleagues the greater the likelihood they will want to support you. Investing in your colleagues could include recognising the resources they need, helping them work through tricky issues, encouraging them to take forward their own personal development and introducing them to other people with whom they might have a shared interest.

Investing in a colleague might be about opening their mind to what is possible going forward. It can be sowing seeds for the longer term. A person I respected suggested when I was 21 that I write a book on freedom and responsibility. It was 34 years later that my first book was published, but a seed had been sown with that suggestion.

Investing in colleagues might be about spending focused half-hours with them to talk through issues. It might include short conversations to acknowledge in a specific way the quality and impact of their contribution. We can invest in someone effectively by encouraging them to realise there is a particular strength or area of potential that is worth developing further.

Investing in colleagues is never about vague platitudes or wishful thinking about the future. It is a purposeful investment of time, an opportunity to make suggestions, and a mutual sharing of learning about what might be possible.

Mustaq recognised that the work his group was doing would not be straightforward for all its members. He was conscious that the estates director could be narrow in his thinking. Mustaq deliberately invested time working with this colleague to help him think through issues from a wider perspective.

Mustaq used a combination of teasing his colleague about his natural preferences and encouraging him to think about the importance of his contribution to the wider success of the university. This combination of teasing, gentle challenge and talking through possibilities began to shift his colleague into a different and more corporate space.

In practice

- Be specific about what investing in your colleagues might mean

- Be deliberate in the way you use the power of the question or the power of suggestion with your colleagues

- Ensure you set aside enough time to invest in colleagues, recognising that a lot can be achieved in a focused half-hour conversation

- See investing in colleagues as a major part of investing in your own future

- Do not assume there will be short-term benefits from investing in colleagues

HOW DO YOU KEEP UP THE MOMENTUM OF A TEAM?

It can be relatively straightforward getting a team to start off with energy, but much more difficult keeping up that momentum.

The idea

Energy levels of teams rise and fall surprisingly quickly. It only takes a couple of reverses, with some members being grumpy, for team morale and commitment to collapse. When a team is being formed its relative newness can be an opportunity for members to say openly what their hopes are and how they want to contribute. Once a team has defined its way of working it can surprisingly quickly become conservative and resist fresh approaches.

Keeping up the momentum of a team depends upon a clear shared desire to reach particular outcomes, alongside a way of working that keeps people interested, engaged and motivated. It is well worth a team leader assessing the momentum level of a team out of ten and then asking why the momentum level has changed in recent weeks and what is needed to put the momentum level up a couple of notches.

Sometimes momentum can rise because the leader has given team members a stiff talking to. More often momentum rises because there is a shared urgency about the endeavour and a clarity about the common purpose and what the team now needs to do to deliver the next step towards ultimate success.

A team's momentum needs to be treated like a fragile vase that has to be carefully looked after. It can be shattered and very difficult to put back together, but a vase that is looked after can hold many different types of flowers. A team's momentum that is looked after can deliver a wide range of outcomes beyond people's expectations.

Mustaq observed a dip in the energy levels of the team after six months. The group was clear on its objectives but beginning to get bogged down on certain details. Mustaq led an open discussion about the momentum of the group in which the inhibitors were shared and an agreement reached about how they could maintain their earlier momentum both as individuals and as a group.

The team talked frankly about a couple of blockages that needed to be addressed, which included overcoming some rigid attitudes about what was possible. The group agreed that every six months they should review their level of momentum and be open about inhibitors and blockages that needed to be worked through.

In practice

- Be dispassionate in assessing the momentum levels of a team

- Encourage open conversation about what keeps the momentum high and what suppresses momentum

- Encourage openness about inhibitors and blockages that need to be addressed

- Ensure regular reviews of the momentum levels and possible inhibitors

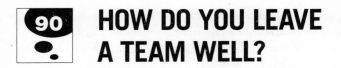

HOW DO YOU LEAVE A TEAM WELL?

LEAVING A TEAM WELL involves ensuring that it continues to be successful after your departure.

The idea

When we move on from leading a team we can be preoccupied with our own next steps. What is just as important is ensuring that the team you are leaving continues to be successful. This does not mean establishing a series of constraints so that the team in the future can only operate in the way you established. You want the team to continue to adapt and thrive.

Leaving a team well depends on how you have built up capabilities within it and whether there is a momentum in the way it works together that will carry it forward to its next phase. You will want to ensure that team members are not over-dependent on you and can switch their allegiance smoothly to the next leader.

The good team leader will recognise that they are not dispensable and will have developed ways of working within the team that are effective when the team leader is absent. Ideally you would have developed a momentum that allows the team to operate well without you, with its effectiveness not dropping during the period of transition to a new leader.

Leaving a team well includes building an agreed understanding of the progress that has been reached by the team at your point of departure. It is always worth a stock-take with a team before you depart so there is an agreement about the outcomes which can be shared with others for the benefit of the team and for you as its team leader. These are points where you want an acknowledgement of what has been delivered under your watch, with some documentation about these conclusions becoming part of your career narrative.

Mustaq did not expect to be moving on from leading this group in the near future, but he was mindful that he needed to grow the confidence of members of the group so that some of them could take over from him if he needed to be away for a period. At regular points he fed back to the University Vice-Chancellor what had been delivered by the group. The combination of building the confidence of those who could succeed him in leading the group and ensuring the Vice-Chancellor knew of the outcomes delivered meant that Mustaq had the personal confidence that he could move on at any point and the group's work would continue unabated.

In practice

- Always invest in your potential successors

- Recognise that you are never indispensable and create ways of working in a team so that it can operate without you

- Never become so tied to a team that you would hate moving on

- Ensure that the team and your contribution to the team is acknowledged in writing at periodic intervals so there is appropriate credit against your name when you move on

SECTION J
ENGAGE WITH THE FUTURE

STAND IN FUTURE POSSIBILITIES

'STANDING IN' THE FUTURE means projecting yourself several years ahead and envisaging the possibilities, so as to be clearer where you want to make your future contribution.

The idea

We can be so absorbed in the present that we do not think constructively about the future. Standing in the future can seem an irrelevant waste of time. There are tasks to be done now and expectations to be met. We do not want to be distracted by thinking about what might be vaguely possible in the future.

If we are too absorbed in the present, we can overlook future possibilities. Eventually we are forced to think beyond the immediate because of circumstances outside our control. When that happens we might find that the world has passed us by and discover that our experience and approach are dated and no longer marketable.

Standing in future possibilities is not about constant daydreaming. It is about creating time and space on a periodic basis to reflect on future possibilities that might be two, five or ten years ahead. Thinking through different potential possibilities enables us to assess what will give us fulfilment, energy and joy. Using our emotions as a barometer can help us rank different alternatives.

When I am coaching individuals I encourage them to think through both obvious and less obvious possibilities. I encourage them to think laterally about how their generic skills could be used in different contexts. I invite them to consider what contribution they can make at a more senior level and whether that would bring a greater sense of fulfilment or anguish.

To enable you to stand in future possibilities it is often useful to invite a friend or colleague to help you work through different options. Someone who knows your capabilities can help stretch your thinking about future possibilities.

Maureen was the Deputy Dean of a cathedral in a busy city. She was engrossed in her work and loved the variety of activities she was involved in. The cathedral was fully engaged in the life of the city. Maureen brushed aside suggestions from colleagues that she might become a Dean of a cathedral or a Bishop in the future.

Maureen had banished ambition as a selfish illusion but her Bishop was persistent that Maureen should think through whether she might, in due course, want to become a Dean of a cathedral or a Bishop. She was persuaded that she needed to develop some of the skills and approaches that would equip her for such a senior leadership role.

In practice

- Be mindful if there are self-limiting beliefs stopping you from exploring future possibilities

- Be willing to set aside some time periodically to envisage yourself in future possibilities

- Observe your emotions as you stand in different possibilities

- Draw in trusted others to help you think through what the future might hold

- Keep assessing whether you are captive to outdated views about your own limitations

RECOGNISE WHAT YOU CAN AND CANNOT CONTROL ABOUT THE FUTURE

BRINGING REALISM ABOUT what you can and cannot control about the future provides a framework within which you can be clearer about what are realistic choices.

The idea

When we seek to engage with future possibilities we can become preoccupied with what lies outside our control. We see limitations in our competences, experiences and personal circumstances. Our mind is flooded with inhibitions and constraints.

We have to force ourselves to think about what we can control rather than what we cannot control. We can control our attitudes and a proportion of our time. We can control our approach to continuing education and training. We can decide we are open to new possibilities, or we might deliberately choose to close our mind to options that might take us outside our comfort zone.

A key starting point in engaging with the future is to be realistic about what you cannot control, including the financial and family commitments that you have entered into and are important to you. If you think about what might capture your imagination and what might inspire you, then some of your self-imposed restrictions might lessen. Most of us can normally find some time for things we really want to do. When we are inspired there is a renewed desire to have more control over our next steps.

Maureen recognised that in a busy job there was much in her diary she could not control. There were cathedral services to lead, committees to chair, people to meet and meetings to attend. If she applied for a senior role she would not be in control of the selection procedure. Choices would be made on whether her skills and approach fitted the particular context well, rather than just being based on an assessment of her strengths. She could not control the geographical location of where possible roles might be available.

Maureen recognised that she could control her attitude to the future in terms of being open to different possibilities. She could set aside a proportion of her time to prepare her narrative about how she would tackle a more senior role. She was willing to spend time work-shadowing different leaders and attend seminars led by leaders from different spheres. She kept up the discipline of reading biographies and reflective pieces about how people had handled demanding situations. Part of the way she kept her own mind open was through encouraging younger people to keep an open mind about future possibilities.

In practice

- Recognise what you cannot control, but double-check whether you are limiting yourself too much

- Beware lest you are captive to self-limiting attitudes

- Be excited about your aspirations and the use of time that you can control

- Celebrate when you have liberated yourself from a closed mind on a particular subject

BE ENTREPRENEURIAL

BEING ENTREPRENEURIAL IS ABOUT reflecting on the competences and experience you bring and their marketability in different contexts.

The idea

We can feel constrained by limited experience. If we have spent our working life as a local government official or a junior manager in an insurance company, or a ward clerk in a hospital, what else can we do with these experiences? Our job might have developed in us skills in running projects, influencing a range of different people, building joint working to solve problems, and organising meetings that reach considered conclusions. We may have developed skills in contributing to committees well and chairing meetings effectively. We may have developed the ability to plan ahead and know how to meet a necessary timescale.

We may have developed an ability to articulate what is happening in a situation, put forward a coherent case and summarise arguments well. We may have developed a skill in drafting clear and persuasive text. We may have built an understanding of different points of view and how best to reach agreed ways forward.

All of us have developed skills that are transferable. Recognising the transferability of our skills is the first step to being entrepreneurial. It is then a matter of describing our skills and experience in a way that is attractive to others so that they can see how we can contribute to delivering outcomes that are most important to them.

Maureen was initially hesitant about whether a Deputy Dean of a cathedral should be entrepreneurial, but she recognised that cathedral leaders needed to be confident in contributing to the life of the city and in deciding how it could extend its influence. She set up lectures and seminars about current issues that had an ethical dimension. She became more willing to use her role and her personality to bring people together and help stretch the thinking of leaders and opinion-formers in the city.

Maureen recognised that she was becoming increasingly entrepreneurial in her role as Deputy Dean. She was an agent for constructive change in the city. She recognised that she could be entrepreneurial in thinking through how she could contribute to both church life and public life if she moved into a more senior role in the Church. She was much more open to taking on leading a civic project on behalf of the whole city. This was an opportunity for her to be entrepreneurial both on behalf of the cathedral and in developing her own leadership experience.

In practice

- Recognise that you do have transferable skills and experience

- Be willing to think through where your skills can be applied on a broader stage

- Recognise which organisations might welcome the type of contribution and experience you can bring

- See being entrepreneurial as a positive choice

BE BOTH FOCUSED AND PHILOSOPHICAL

GETTING THE BALANCE RIGHT between being focused and philosophical enables you to explore possibilities in depth without becoming too emotionally attached to them.

The idea

There is often a tendency to be vague in thinking of the future. There might be a myriad of possibilities. You think it is not worth working through possibilities because the right opportunities will never arise, or there will be external factors that result in none of the possibilities coming to fruition.

It is right to be philosophical that life is unpredictable and you cannot plan for the future with any degree of certainty. But the risk is that we allow inevitable uncertainty about the future to limit the energy we put into exploring future possibilities. We do not want to create disappointments for ourselves or go up blind alleys. We think that being too focused on some future possibilities will inevitably leave us disappointed.

Being focused means thinking through how our generic skills might apply in different future possibilities. It means restraining our natural hesitancy. Seeking the advice of trusted others could help us consider the type of opportunities that others identify as appropriate for our skills and temperament. Asking a trusted other to be in conversation with you about opportunities and risks and how people might perceive your contribution can help clarify thinking about future possibilities.

It is worth focusing on what would energise you about different possibilities and what is the distinctive contribution that you can make. If you focus on the outcomes that you might be able to help deliver, it can help you assess which future possibilities would fully engage your commitment.

Maureen recognised that the efforts she put into city-wide initiatives and into her own personal development needed to be worthwhile in themselves. It was important that whatever she focused on was consistent with where she wanted to add value and contribute. If they led to an interesting future role that would be a worthwhile outcome. Some current activities were fully worthwhile even if they had no effect for her in terms of longer-term advancement. She recognised that long-term advancement was not the prime driver for her, and recognised the value of focusing on activities or learning that were worthwhile in themselves and could open up future possibilities.

In practice

- Be clear where you want to place your focus and be willing to say no to other possibilities

- When you focus on an activity be mindful of both your short-term contribution and your long-term learning

- Recognise that many things you do will not lead anywhere and be ready to be philosophical about that

- Review periodically whether you are focusing on the right type of activities and learning, or whether it is time to move on

95 TRUST YOUR INTUITIVE JUDGEMENT

REMEMBER THAT YOUR intuitive judgement is based on your years of experience. It is right to test it and take it seriously.

The idea

Sometimes we might have apparently random ideas about what we might engage with in the future. Curiosity might have been sparked by a conversation or something we came across in the media. Most of these ideas we will probably want to dismiss after relatively brief reflection.

Sometimes our imagination is genuinely caught by something that appeals to values and interests within us. When I was at a weekend conference in 2001 I met someone who talked to me about their work as an executive coach. I was intrigued by what they said and began to sense that executive coaching was something that could capture my imagination. When I described this conversation to my wife, Frances, she had a strong intuitive sense that one day I would move into executive coaching as a second career. I made that move a couple of years later.

We are a mixture of values and experiences drawn from our family heritage, our cultural background and our mix of work, life and community experiences. Sometimes these experiences and qualities reinforce each other and equip us for future possibilities. Leading a sports team and a project team at work develops confidence and competences within us that can equip us for a range of different team leadership roles.

There might be a latent desire to apply these competences to working in a different part of the country or world. This might result from looking through 'rose-tinted glasses', or it might be that deep within us there is an association with or an attraction to a very different environment. These notions are always worth exploring rather than dismissing outright.

Maureen had grown up in the north of England and was now working in southern England. There was a hankering in her to return to the north. She reflected on whether this was purely a legacy from her childhood or whether there was a latent desire in her to contribute to the community and spiritual life of northern communities.

Maureen did not dwell on this intuitive judgement. She held it in her mind as she knew at some stage she would move on from her current post. She wanted to be open to the possibility of returning to the north of England without being constrained by the belief that this was inevitable. She recognised that other contexts could capture her imagination. It was wrong to constrain herself in thinking of future options, but it was right to be open to an intuitive sense of excitement about unknown and unthought-of possibilities.

In practice

- Recognise when you have an intuitive sense of what the future might hold

- Reflect seriously on and assess intuitive responses to options others mention to you

- Be open to triangulating your intuitive reactions with trusted others

- Keep an open heart and mind about the future so you can be accepting of new and unexpected ideas

96 DON'T TAKE YOURSELF TOO SERIOUSLY

You HAVE TO LEARN to laugh at yourself or else you risk becoming racked with disappointment and guilt.

The idea

Sometimes we believe we have such a unique mix of experiences and skills that we are ideally suited to the particular job we are applying for. It is right to have a clear narrative setting out the strengths you bring and the contribution you would make in a particular role. But it is dangerous to think of yourself as uniquely qualified for a role as this can lead to an arrogance that will diminish rather than enhance your prospects.

As we explore future possibilities it is right to take them seriously and look at the options from different perspectives, but it is equally important that we do not take ourselves too seriously. All of us have 'feet of clay'. We have all made mistakes and have our vulnerabilities. We are all far from perfect. So how can we be uniquely qualified for any role?

A crucial balance is needed between a purposeful, clear narrative of who we are and what we bring, alongside a lightness about our strengths and limitations. If we can laugh at ourselves and our foibles we can enter discussions about our future with a smile on our face and a lightness in our heart. If we are ultra-serious about ourselves and our intent we are quite likely to repel rather than attract the people whom we want to be our advocates.

It is right to be serious-minded when exploring opportunities and risks. We want to bring clarity of intent in order to be convincing that we can deliver outcomes. What is needed is a seriousness that draws people in because of our resolve and commitment, and not a seriousness that turns people away because they feel unable to engage with us.

Maureen recognised that because she was an ordained priest there was likely to be a deference to her and an expectation that she would be serious and probably humourless. She deliberately built rapport with people by seeking to find areas where she could talk with them in a light-hearted way. She was willing to share stories and engage people at a human level.

Maureen knew that if she was over-serious in her role she would not win the engagement of other partners in the city. She recognised that coming over within the cathedral context as over-serious would be both unhelpful and contrary to her values. Whenever she had a substantive conversation with someone she wanted them to move on with serious intent and a lightness of heart.

In practice

- Recognise the early warning signs that you are in danger of becoming over-serious

- Be aware of when you may be taking yourself too seriously and understand how it can damage your interactions with others

- Seek a balance between having serious intent and a lightness of heart

- Be willing to laugh at yourself and recognise when you are taking yourself too seriously

97

BE READY TO BE SURPRISED

LOOKING FORWARD it is right to be focused and at the same time open to being surprised. It is the unexpected that can sometimes inspire you the most.

The idea

When I left Government service after 32 years I moved deliberately into executive coaching. Following an initial conversation at a week-end conference in 2001 my imagination had been caught by the possibility of coaching work. After a couple of years I was ready to move into my second career, which has been enormously fulfilling over the 13 years since.

What took me by surprise was the opportunity to write books. This is the 22nd book written over a period of 12 years. I look back with sur-prise about this move into writing books. What enabled me to make this transition was years of dictating notes of meetings, submissions and papers to very tight timescales. My first career had developed in me skills that I had not appreciated could be transferred into writing a couple of books a year.

As you think about the future, be open to being surprised. You may have latent gifts or capabilities that have been honed in previous spheres that are more transferable than you might have realised. In your current world these qualities may be taken for granted. In a future world these qualities might be exactly what people are search-ing for.

As you explore future possibilities it is worth asking people in different spheres what qualities they observe in you. Their comments might not always be what you expect. If you are good at contributing in meetings or writing reports or building partnerships, these qualities might be much more appreciated in a new world than you imagine. On the other hand do not be too surprised if what you think is a unique quality in yourself is viewed as irrelevant or out of date.

Maureen was pleasantly surprised by the feedback from city councillors she worked with on a regeneration project. They described her as skilled in building relationships and able to identify the most important considerations. They saw her bringing both human empathy and intellectual astuteness. Maureen was greatly encouraged by comments from politicians who had no particular interest in church matters. This encouragement helped her recognise that she could make a contribution on a wider platform and build constructive working relationships with a wide mix of different people.

In practice

- Remember when you have been surprised by other people's positive comments about you – what did you learn from the comments?

- When have you been taken by surprise by your own reflections or contribution – what did you learn from that reaction?

- How open are you to putting yourself into a situation where you might be taken by surprise about what the future might hold for you?

- What are the skills you have that others most appreciate that could be transferred into other contexts?

98

BEWARE THE BLINKERS

A BLINKERED APPROACH can help us survive and focus, but if we are too blinkered we do not identify all the opportunities and risks.

The idea

The runner keeps going by focusing on the finishing line; they blot out the cheering crowds from view. The architect knows there is a deadline for producing the required plans; they blot out other distractions so the deadline is met. The executive coach knows that if they are to be fully present with an individual or group they have to block out all distractions; the good coach learns to put on firm blinkers so they are not distracted.

We all do and should use blinkers in a deliberate way so we focus well, engage fully and bring tasks to completion. But blinkers can be as dangerous in some situations as they are helpful in others. The accountant focused on submitting the financial results to the auditor by a specific date might be in danger of being so blinkered that they ignore information that might throw them off course. The accountant needs to take the blinkers off so they see fully the consequences of some partial information and the risks that might be lurking beneath.

When we are too blinkered we want to dismiss information that is contrary to our expectations. We do not want to hear views from people we suspect are critics. We are reluctant to think about what might go wrong as it is unsettling.

Sometimes we have to take the blinkers off so we see ourselves and our future unalloyed. This can be painful but the result is greater clarity about what matters most to us going forward. With the blinkers off we then make decisions by conscious choice and not by default.

Maureen felt more confident in meetings in a cathedral setting than in a city or community setting. She felt that she did not necessarily have anything interesting to say on wider issues. But gradually she took the blinkers off, partially because she enjoyed contributing on a wider range of topics, and also due to positive affirmation from community leaders, politicians and business people.

Maureen increasingly recognised there were a range of perspectives on inner-city problems which she wanted to engage with. No longer was she blinkered with one particularly view. Because she understood more where others were coming from, her influence became more effective.

In practice

- When have blinkers been helpful to you in enabling you to deliver key outcomes?

- When have you been too blinkered in your approach?

- What are the blinkers you want to remove so that you are more open to engaging with a variety of perspectives?

- How readily can you describe your own blinkers so that you can put them on or remove them at will?

99 KNOW YOUR SOURCES OF RESILIENCE

KNOWING YOUR SOURCES OF resilience is crucial for survival and for equipping yourself for future opportunities.

The idea

Your level of resilience needs to be commensurate with the pressures in your current role and your wider life responsibilities. There is a risk that our resilience levels merely keep up with the expectations currently upon us. The ideal is to build your resilience so there is capacity for you to be able to take on further responsibilities.

Resilience is all about our physical, mental, emotional and spiritual wellbeing. When we are resilient we are able to be fully absorbed in a situation one minute and detached from it the next. Resilience is one of the most precious gifts for any manager or leader.

Building resilience will be about physical exertion, being mentally engaged in a range of different activities, knowing what emotionally sustains us, and spiritually having a clear perspective on what matters most to us in our lives.

Most of us are in danger of operating at the maximum level of our resilience. Once we have built up a store of resilience we then deploy it. Perhaps the ideal is to build up your resilience so there is always some 'rattle space' or spare capacity so that we are not operating at the extremes of our equilibrium.

It can be worth asking, 'What is the level of resilience I will need in whatever I do next?' and then building up your repertoire of approaches to sustaining your resilience in advance of taking on bigger responsibilities.

Maureen knew that she could be over-absorbed in the day-to-day responsibilities at the cathedral. She lived in the precincts of the cathedral and could go for days without any serious physical exercise. She disciplined herself to go for a run three times a week, to read books well away from theology, to join a group of serious walkers and to go to the theatre on a regular basis.

Maureen sought to be increasingly disciplined in the use of her time. She was conscious which activities gave her energy and which sapped her energy. She was much more willing to ration her time with different people. She kept the meetings she was chairing more focused and ended them on time. She brought greater structure to the way she organised her life, with more protected time for other activities. She felt much less drained as a consequence of these decisions and much more influential in discussions.

In practice

- Who do you observe as particularly resilient and what can you learn from them?

- In what situations have you been at your most resilient and what do you take forward from that experience?

- What do you need to do to build your resilience further in terms of your physical, intellectual, emotional and spiritual wellbeing?

- How can you create 'rattle space' so that you are not constantly running from activity to activity and getting over-tired?

- When can you say no and take a break?

100 ENJOY THE JOURNEY

IT IS IMPORTANT that we enjoy the journey, whatever the outcome.

The idea

You may or may not build the success you want. You may or may not be successful in the eyes of other people. Most of what we deliver in life we can brand as either a success or a failure. The pessimist will see what they did as a parent as a failure. The optimistic will see the outcomes of their parenting as success. The truth is that our children are formed through a combination of what we did right, what was less good, and the children's own decisions. As we look back we can describe an event that went wrong as a terrible failure or as crucial to our building clarity about what success means going forward.

Enjoying the journey is not about self-indulgence. It is about sitting lightly so that we can recognise when we have been down a blind alley and when a decision turned out for the best. The long-distance runner will experience tough, painful moments alongside moments of ecstasy when they travel rapidly downhill. Our journeys as we seek to build success will be a cacophony of experiences. Sometimes we will feel let down by others and by ourselves. On other occasions we will feel we have done ourselves justice and been far more effective than we had anticipated.

Our definition of success is likely to have changed during our journey. It may well now be more about developing other people and enjoying their success than being preoccupied with our own success. We may well be amused by our previous blinkered ambitions and sit more lightly to our hopes for the future. On the other hand, we are likely to be just as focused on where we can make a difference and see potential for a contribution that will give us personal satisfaction.

Maureen was both humbled and delighted when she was told that she was now seen as a serious candidate for Dean or Bishop posts. She felt both daunted and excited. She knew that if she went for either type of post her resolve and resilience would be tested, but she felt at peace with this possibility. She wanted to enjoy the next steps in her journey whatever they were. She was ready to keep building up her experience so that she could become a plausible candidate for either of these roles.

Maureen was very conscious that her prime focus should not be looking to fill a more senior post. It was her principal role to be looking after the range of people who entered through the door of the cathedral. Her credibility depended on winning the confidence of parishioners and people across the city. She recognised that her role was similar to many other potential leaders: she had to be both fully engaged with the day-to-day and contribute fully to long-term strategic issues.

In practice

- Recognise and celebrate the journey you have been on

- Be amused by the dated images of success you were attached to in the past

- Keep enjoying each part of the journey, reframing each negative experience as part of your continuous learning

- Celebrate the ups and downs and see success as surviving as well as thriving

BOOKS BY DR PETER SHAW

Mirroring Jesus as Leader. Cambridge: Grove, 2004.

Conversation Matters: How to engage effectively with one another. London: Continuum, 2005.

The Four Vs of Leadership: Vision, values, value-added, and vitality. Chichester: Capstone, 2006.

Finding Your Future: The second time around. London: Darton, Longman and Todd, 2006.

Business Coaching: Achieving practical results through effective engagement. Chichester: Capstone, 2007 (co-authored with Robin Linnecar).

Making Difficult Decisions: How to be decisive and get the business done. Chichester: Capstone, 2008.

Deciding Well: A Christian perspective on making decisions as a leader. Vancouver: Regent College Publishing, 2009.

Raise Your Game: How to succeed at work. Chichester: Capstone, 2009.

Effective Christian Leaders in the Global Workplace. Colorado Springs: Authentic/Paternoster, 2010.

Defining Moments: Navigating through business and organisational life. Basingstoke: Palgrave/Macmillan, 2010.

The Reflective Leader: Standing still to move forward. Norwich: Canterbury Press, 2011 (co-authored with Alan Smith).

Thriving In Your Work: How to be motivated and do well in challenging times. London: Marshall Cavendish, 2011.

Getting the Balance Right: Leading and managing well. Singapore: Marshall Cavendish, 2013.

Leading in Demanding Times. Cambridge: Grove, 2013 (co-authored with Graham Shaw).

The Emerging Leader: Stepping up in leadership. Norwich: Canterbury Press, 2013 (co-authored with Colin Shaw).

100 Great Personal Impact Ideas. Singapore: Marshall Cavendish, 2013.

100 Great Coaching Ideas. Singapore: Marshall Cavendish, 2014.

Celebrating Your Senses. Delhi: ISPCK, 2014.

Sustaining Leadership: Renewing your strength and sparkle. Norwich: Canterbury Press, 2014.

100 Great Team Effectiveness Ideas. Singapore: Marshall Cavendish, 2015.

Wake Up and Dream: Stepping into your future. Norwich: Canterbury Press, 2015.

100 Great Building Success Ideas. Singapore: Marshall Cavendish, 2016.

FORTHCOMING BOOKS

The Reluctant Leader. Norwich: Canterbury Press, 2016 (co-authored with Hilary Douglas).

ABOUT THE AUTHOR

DR PETER SHAW works with individuals, teams and groups to help them grow their strengths and tackle demanding issues confidently. His objective is to help individuals and teams clarify the vision of who they want to be, the values that are driving them, the value-added they want to bring and their sources of vitality.

His work on how leaders step up successfully into demanding leadership roles and sustain that success was recognised with the award of a Doctorate by Publication from the University of Chester in 2011.

Peter is a founding partner of Praesta Partners, an international specialist coaching business. His clients enjoy frank, challenging conversations leading to fresh thinking and new insights. It is the dynamic nature of the conversations that provides a stimulus for creating reflection and new action. He often works with Chief Executives and Board Members taking on new roles and leading major organisational change. Peter has worked with a wide range of leadership teams as they tackle new challenges.

Peter has worked with Chief Executives and senior teams in a range of different sectors and countries. He has led workshops on such themes as 'Riding the Rapids', 'Seizing the Future', 'Thriving in your Work', 'Being an Agile Leader' and 'Building Resilience' across six continents.

Peter has held a wide range of Board posts covering finance, personnel, policy, communications and delivery. He worked in five UK Government Departments (Treasury, Education, Employment, Environment and Transport). He delivered major national changes such as radically different pay arrangements for teachers, a huge expansion in nursery education and employment initiatives which helped bring unemployment below a million.

He led the work on the merger of the UK Government Departments of Education and Employment. As Finance Director General he managed a £40bn budget and introduced radical changes in funding and accountability arrangements. In three Director General posts he led strategic development and implementation in major policy areas. In 2000 he was awarded a CB by the Queen for his contribution to public service.

Peter has written a sequence of 22 influential leadership books. He is a Visiting Professor of Leadership Development at Newcastle University Business School and a Visiting Professor in the Business, Enterprise and Lifelong Learning Department at the University of Chester. He has worked with senior staff at Brighton University and postgraduate students at Warwick University Business School and lectures regularly at Regent College in Vancouver. He is a Professorial Fellow at St John's College, Durham University. He was awarded an Honorary Doctorate (Doctor of Civil Law) by Durham University in 2015 for 'outstanding service to public life and the Council of St John's College'.

Peter is a Reader (licensed lay minister) in the Anglican Church and has worked with senior church leaders in the UK, North America and Asia. His inspiration comes from long-distance walks: he has completed 21 long-distance walks in the UK, including the St Cuthbert's Way, the South Downs Way, the Yorkshire Wolds Way, the Yorkshire Dales Way, the Ribble Way, the Speyside Way, the St Oswald's Way and the Great Glen Way. Peter and his wife, Frances, have three grown-up children who are all married, and a growing number of grandchildren.